THE HISTORIC
SHOPS & RESTAURANTS
OF BOSTON
✦

The Historic Shops
& Restaurants of
BOSTON

PHYLLIS MÉRAS

THE LITTLE BOOKROOM · NEW YORK

© 2007 Phyllis Méras
Design: Louise Fili Ltd

Library of Congress Cataloging-in-Publication Data
Méras, Phyllis. The historic shops and restaurants of Boston :
a guide to century-old establishments in the city / By Phyllis Méras. p. cm.
ISBN-13: 978-1-892145-44-4 (alk. paper)
ISBN-10: 1-892145-44-8 (alk. paper)
1. Shopping—Massachusetts—Boston—Guidebooks.
2. Restaurants—Massachusetts—Boston—Guidebooks. I. Title.
TX336.5.M4M47 2007 917.4.'610444—dc22 2006029686

Cover: Union Oyster House, courtesy of Union Oyster House

Published by The Little Bookroom
1755 Broadway, 5th floor
New York NY 10019
T (212) 293-1643 F (212) 333-5374
editorial@littlebookroom.com
www.littlebookroom.com

CONTENTS

FOR FRANCES
FOR DECADES OF WISE AND
PATIENT COUNSEL
✦

INTRODUCTION

*F*ROM ITS VERY BEGINNING IN 1630, BOSTON WAS A BUSTLING PORT WITH ENERGETIC tradespeople clustered around its docks. In 1996, conscious of this enterprising past, the city inaugurated a Boston Business Heritage Project that pinpointed city businesses that had existed and prospered down through the centuries. Nearly 200 were found that were more than a century old—some had been established 200 years ago. Not all of these have survived in this last decade, but many have, and their stories are recounted in this book.

Among the oldest of these are restaurants and taverns near what was once Boston's port. The Bell in Hand Tavern on its cobblestone street was serving rum to sailors and dock hands in 1795; the Union Oyster House and Durgin-Park have been offering meals since the 1820s. Lawyer-orator Daniel Webster is said to have washed down his oysters on the half-shell with tumblers of rum and water then, while in this century, Brookline-born President John F. Kennedy enjoyed lobster dinners in the Oyster House's upstairs dining room.

In the heart of old Boston—the great fire of 1872 notwithstanding—a number of businesses have survived. Nearby towns, such as Concord and Lexington, Salem and Milton, are rich in historic businesses as well as history. Here are inns that have welcomed guests since the eighteenth century, a candy shop still making the same confections that have been stirred in its pots since the early days of the nineteenth century, a cracker factory that made hardtack for the Union Army.

In this book, which covers not only downtown Boston but its outlying districts and its neighboring towns, are hardware stores, bookshops, tobacconists, fishmongers, grocers, and what is said to be the nation's oldest family-run barber shop. There is a shoe company and a flag company and locksmiths, florists, bakeries, clothing stores, art galleries, and music stores. Founded by Puritans as it was, Boston has always taken its social obligations seriously and among its long-standing enterprises are animal rescue missions and a thrift shop for those in need.

Through the years, immigrants from many lands have settled in the city and established their own communities. Often restaurants and bakeries are in second- and third-generation Italian hands; taverns and stone-cutting yards are Irish-American-owned; clothing stores owned by the descendants of Jewish immigrants. Occasionally, these businesses still occupy the same site where they opened a century or more ago. More often, as real estate values have escalated in the city and neighborhoods have changed, they have moved to new locations, but their owners, proudly cognizant of the past as Bostonians tend to be, still offer the same quality goods and services that their forefathers did.

PHYLLIS MÉRAS
Martha's Vineyard, December 2006

ART GALLERIES & SOCIETIES

✦

COPLEY SOCIETY OF ART

158 NEWBURY STREET, BOSTON
☎ (617) 536-5049
🚊 MBTA GREEN LINE TO COPLEY
TUESDAY-SATURDAY 11AM TO 6PM;
SUNDAY NOON TO 5PM

✦

*T*ODAY COPLEY SQUARE IN BOSTON'S BACK BAY IS ONE OF THE CITY'S MOST SOPHISTICATED, upscale areas, crowded with fashion shops, gourmet restaurants, and art galleries, so it's hard to imagine that in the early 1800s this was a polluted, smelly mudflat. The transformation began when the Back Bay area was filled in and developed between 1857 and 1886. Among the churches, cultural institutions, and homes that were built was the Museum of Fine Arts that opened on July 4 in 1876, in what came to be aptly named Copley Square. John Singleton Copley, considered the foremost artist in colonial America, is known for his powerful portraits of prominent Bostonians, including one of Paul Revere holding a silver teapot.

In 1879, a group of enthusiastic young graduates of the newly established school of the Museum of Fine Arts Boston organized the Copley Society to continue to paint together, socialize, and exhibit their work. In addition to its art, the society was well known in its first fifty years for its extravagant revels and costume parties, which attracted members of Boston's cultural set as well as art lovers from far away. The society gained considerable renown, too, for its exhibitions of the works of James McNeill Whistler, John Singer Sargent, and Claude Monet.

The group had no real home until 1881, when the group remodeled a former roller skating rink on Clarendon Street. Named the Grundmann Studio Building after the Museum School's first teacher, Otto Grundmann, it held studios and exhibition spaces. The Copley Society stayed at Copley Square until 1920, when the building was demolished to make way for Stuart Street. After several moves, the society found its current home in 1957 in an 1899 brownstone on Newbury Street—the city's European-style center of art galleries, coiffeurs, and boutiques.

Today, the society has 600 artist members—a far cry from the handful who started it more than a century ago. The artists are selected by their peers based on the quality of their work. The building has two galleries. In the lower level, smaller works starting at about $100 are for sale. In the street level gallery larger pieces may sell for as much as $60,000.

GIUST GALLERY

105 SALEM STREET, WOBURN
☎ (781) 933-2455
🚃 MBTA ORANGE OR BLUE LINE TO STATE,
THEN BUS #134
MONDAY-FRIDAY 8:30AM TO 4:30PM;
APPOINTMENT PREFERRED

✦

*W*ANDER INTO THE BUSTLING GIUST GALLERY AND YOU WILL FIND ARTISAN EMPLOYEES surrounded, as they work, by busts of philosophers and poets and generals, as well as life-size and more-than-life-size creations in plaster and bronze, used as decorations for private gardens as well as public projects. Current owners and sculptors Robert Shure and his wife, Kathleen, have reincarnated the old Chickey studio that opened in 1835, filling it with busts and statues of the studio's heyday in the 1890s and early 1900s.

Francis Chickey and Company, on School Street in downtown Boston, produced plaster casts of classical statues to decorate the halls of schools and libraries, as was the custom of the day. The founder was Francesco Cicchi, an Italian master craftsman from Tuscany, an area noted for its fine casting and stonemasonry. Cicchi named his gallery after his

Americanized name.

In 1847, Chickey joined with another craftsman, Paul A. Garey, to form Chickey and Garey. After Chickey's death, his partner kept only the Garey name. At the turn of the nineteenth century, popular items in the company catalogue included a plaster reproduction of Lincoln Memorial sculptor Daniel Chester French's bust of Ralph Waldo Emerson, one of Boston sculptor Cyrus Dallin's Oliver Wendell Holmes, and Jean Antoine Houdon's George Washington.

Joining the company as an apprentice in 1895 had been Pietro Paulo Caproni, also from Tuscany. Not too long afterward, Pietro and his brother Emilio bought the business, renaming it P.P. Caproni & Brother, Statuary Makers and publishing a catalogue of their plaster cast reproductions of antique, medieval, and modern sculptures. They modernized their plaster cast collection with works by such European sculptors as nineteenth-century Dane Bertol Thorvaldsen and eighteenth-century Italian neo-classicist Antonio Canova. In 1902 their casts of statues related to music were selected to fill niches at Symphony Hall, where they may be seen to this day. By 1913, Caproni plaster casts of statuary were in the halls of Harvard, Cornell, Princeton, Dartmouth, Andover and Exeter academies, the

[15]

Detroit Museum of Art, and the University of Texas, among others.

But about the time of World War II, enthusiasm for classical sculpture reproductions declined. In 1939, the director of the Museum of Fine Arts informed Caproni Galleries Inc. (then the company's name) that the primary function of a great museum was to display original art and that eliminating casts was a growing tendency among museums. In the 1950s, much of Harvard University's plaster cast collection was destroyed by architecture students at a "party" given by Walter Gropius. They were, they said, seeking to break with classical tradition and even inspired something of a backlash. Similarly, students at the Pennsylvania Academy of Fine Arts tossed part of its Caproni collection down an elevator shaft.

The Caproni company's heyday was clearly over. But another artistic Italian immigrant, Lino Giust, who worked in Boston as a terrazzo setter after his arrival in 1953, saved the collection from disappearing altogether. Having heard the story of the Caproni brothers, in 1971 he bought the Washington Street building the firm had last occupied, along with what remained of its contents. Much of the statuary was in pieces. Nonetheless, enamored of his find, Giust began to learn how to make casts and to restore what he could. He also went in search of Caproni works in buildings scheduled for demolition and acquired them. He showed what he had acquired in a gallery on Newbury Street in the 1970s and 1980s. But by 1997, after thirty years, he was ready to pass on the business to someone else.

Today, under Robert and Kathleen Shure, the Giust Gallery has recreated Parthenon sculptures for Caesar's Palace in Las Vegas and cast bronzes of Christopher Columbus, Venus de Milo, Benjamin Franklin, and Calvin Coolidge for civic projects throughout the country. Closer to home, the reproductions they have made and cast in bronze in Boston include portraits of suffragettes that decorate the State House and the relief of Boston Red Sox player Ted Williams that stands at the entrance to the new Ted Williams Tunnel. And it is this historic company that repaired the gilded grasshopper weathervane that stirs with the wind above Boston's Faneuil Hall.

THE SOCIETY OF ARTS & CRAFTS

175 NEWBURY STREET, BOSTON
☎ (617) 266-1810
🚇 MBTA GREEN LINE TO COPLEY; OR
MBTA ORANGE LINE TO BACK BAY
MONDAY-SATURDAY 10AM TO 6PM,
SUNDAY NOON TO 5PM

✦

*N*INETEENTH-CENTURY BOSTON TOOK TO THE ARTS AND CRAFTS MOVEMENT OF Victorian England with enthusiasm. When craftsman-designer William Morris, in reaction to the Industrial Revolution, urged a return to the handmade decorative arts of the Middle Ages, Boston's leading architects, designers, and educators immediately embraced his cause on this side of the Atlantic. Boston became the gateway for the movement in the United States.

In 1897, they organized an exhibition of contemporary crafts held at Copley Hall in Copley Square (previously Art Square, but renamed for Boston painter John Singleton Copley in 1883). The exhibition attracted throngs. More than 1,000 objects made by 160 craftsmen and craftswomen were displayed. Included, among others, were picture frames, wallpaper, draperies, mural decorations, stone carvings, engravings, and wrought iron. The opening of the exhibition was the great social event of the year, attended by Boston's Brahmins as well as by artists and educators from all over New England and as far away as New York and Philadelphia. Clearly, there were artists aplenty who longed to create and a public that responded to what they fashioned.

And so, in 1900, The Society of Arts and Crafts, established to further this new arts movement, opened a Handicraft Shop on Somerset Street near the State House. The handcrafted objects sold were jury-selected. By 1902 the society was also publishing its own magazine, *Handicraft*, and had moved its shop to 9 Park Street, a more central location, in hopes of increasing sales.

But the Depression came, leading to another move—this one to 32 Newbury Street in the Back Bay business area. The store remained there until 1975, when it moved to the brownstone and brick building at 175 Newbury Street it now occupies.

Here, on the second floor, changing exhibits of jury-selected objects in clay, glass, fiber, metal, and wood are held. Downstairs, other jury-chosen objects crafted in the same materials are available for purchase. These include ceramics, woven goods, hollowware, blown glass and glass beads, jewelry, dyed and painted fabric handbags, scarves, and clothes.

VOSE GALLERIES OF BOSTON, INC.

238 NEWBURY ST., BOSTON

☎ (617) 536-6176

🚇 MBTA GREEN LINE TO COPLEY OR HYNES/ICA

MONDAY-FRIDAY 9:30AM TO 5:30PM;

SATURDAY 10:30AM TO 5:30PM

✦

*I*N THE 1840S, PROVIDENCE, R.I., SHOE MANU-
FACTURER JOSEPH VOSE DECIDED TO BRANCH
out into the art business, and bought a gallery in that
city. Four decades later, his son, Seth, opened another
gallery on Tremont Street in Boston's expanding
Back Bay. The Back Bay was a relatively new part of
the city, having been created by filling in the Charles
River bay with gravel from surrounding hills, a pro-
cess that took from 1857 to 1886. The streets of this
new part of the city were laid out in the fashion of
the boulevards of Paris.

When Seth Vose opened his gallery, he repre-
sented such American artists as Martin Johnson
Head and Albert Bierstadt. He then began importing works by Theodore Rousseau, Jean-Francois Mil-
let, and the French Barbizon School artists. The first
shipment Seth received from Paris included a Jean-
Louis Gericault full frontal nude of a blacksmith.

Proper Bostonian that he was, he had the painting cut in half at the blacksmith's hips. Only then did he feel it was appropriate to sell the top half to the wife of the president of the Museum of Fine Arts. He stowed the lower half away, out of public sight, in his warehouse.

In the 1920s, Seth's son, Robert, moved the gallery to a four-story building he had constructed in fashionable Copley Square. Boston papers called it the finest gallery space in America. The gallery moved to smaller quarters during the Depression, and Vose Galleries now occupies a red-brick brownstone close by on Newbury Street, in the Back Bay area.

The present owners are Abbot (Bill) and Robert III (Terry), sons of Robert Jr. It was Robert Jr. who, years after his grandfather had sold the Gericault painting to the MFA, discovered the lower half and offered it to the museum so they could have the whole painting.

Today gallery-goers climb stone steps and pass through a blue-gray paneled vestibule to view nineteenth-century American maritime scenes and American Impressionist works by Maurice Prendergast and Childe Hassam, strolling through the premises as if it were still a private home of Victorian time. Sometimes art might be propped against a wall. Sometimes a painting might be hung beside a grandfather clock or leaning against a wing-backed chair in one of the rooms at the top of the creaking paneled stairs.

Three floors of gallery space house about 800 paintings, although not all are displayed at one time. Vose specializes in nineteenth- and twentieth-century American works but carries paintings by a few living artists as well. Prices range from $1,000 to more than $1,000,000. Snapshots of some of the works the gallery has sold over the years are displayed on the vestibule wall, including a Thomas Gainsborough sold to the Museum of Fine Arts, a Joshua Reynolds sold to the Huntington Gallery in California, and a William Turner that now is the property of the Wadsworth Atheneum in Hartford.

BARBERSHOPS

✦

GEORGE'S BARBER SHOP

59 JACKSON STREET, SAUGUS
☎ (781) 233-0289
🚌 MBTA BUS #426 OR #426W TO
CLIFTONDALE SQUARE
TUESDAY-SATURDAY 8AM TO 4:30PM

✦

*I*N THE SEVENTEENTH CENTURY, SAUGUS, WITH ITS RICH SUPPLY OF BOG IRON ORE FROM THE bed of the Saugus River, was the site of one of the first colonial iron works, producing as much as ten tons a week. Some of this iron was turned into cast iron pots and pans on the spot; more often it became wrought iron bars that were sent back to England, sold to local blacksmiths, or flattened and cut into rods from which nails were sliced. The Saugus iron works was an expensive, sophisticated operation with a blast furnace, a forge, and a rolling mill. The ironworkers were hired from England and they were paid high wages for the inconvenience of working in the colonies. But there was also stiff competition from England in iron ore production and by 1670, production was stopped. Even without the iron works, Saugus, a section of Lynn until 1815, continued to prosper. The surrounding land was fertile and inviting for farming, and until well into the twentieth century it was this rural aspect of the community that attracted many, including a young Italian immigrant, Thomas George Moriello.

Moriello first settled in Boston's North End at the end of the nineteenth century, but he found it crowded—too much like the busy Naples he had left behind. Saugus, with dairy and vegetable farms in its surrounding countryside and a sizable Italian population, was where he opened his barbershop, erecting a red and white barber pole on Cliftondale Square in 1902.

His son, George Rocco Moriello, later operated the shop. Today, two of George's grandsons and two great-grandsons man the four barber chairs. Following time-honored custom, the chair nearest the door is the chair of the most senior barber. Today, George's Barber Shop is the oldest in the United States that remains in the founder's family.

Neither shaves nor shampoos are given at George's—just haircuts—and there are no appointments at this little shop with its black- and white-tile floor, sports pictures on the walls, and business cards printed on poker chips. Although the shop has moved five times since its founding, and the farmland that so attracted Moriello has been gobbled up by development, George's Barber Shop has never left Cliftondale Square.

LA FLAMME BARBER SHOP
OF HARVARD SQUARE

21 DUNSTER STREET, CAMBRIDGE

☎ (617) 354-8377

🚆 MBTA RED LINE TO HARVARD SQUARE

MONDAY, TUESDAY, SATURDAY 7AM TO 6PM;

WEDNESDAY-FRIDAY 7AM TO 7PM

✦

*T*HE HANDSOME DANA CHAMBERS BUILDING
WAS JUST A YEAR OLD IN 1898 WHEN ARTHUR
E. La Flamme opened his barbershop on the ground
floor. Its elegant facade, embellished with terra cotta
medallions and flowers, appealed to the French
Canadian barber, so he furnished his shop in keeping
with those surroundings. The floor-to-ceiling mirrors facing the barber chairs were set in mahogany
frames, the knobs and drawer pulls on his cabinets
were brass, and for counters, nothing less than marble would do.

Of the nine swiveling barber chairs in use today,
all but one are those Arthur La Flamme installed
(and the one that isn't is old, too). The mirrors and
cabinets he chose are still in place, as is the 1887 cash
register from the National Cash Register Company
of Dayton, Ohio, and the porcelain shampoo sink.
The windows that front Dunster Street are floor-to-

ceiling, just as they always have been.

The La Flamme Barber Shop has had only three owners in its 108-year history. When Arthur La Flamme retired, James Lambari took over. Twenty-two years ago, George Papalimberis, who at the time owned other barbershops in Central Square and on Brattle Street, bought it, and continues to protect and maintain the high ceilings, gleaming mirrors, and hanging light fixtures that give La Flamme its turn-of-the-nineteenth-century elegance.

In Brief

PHIL'S BARBER SHOP, 2091A CENTRE STREET, WEST ROXBURY. Although Dan Lourenco, who has owned this shop since 1973, isn't sure of the historical particulars, he knows his shop is more than a century old. In 1998, the Boston Business Heritage Project honored it as one of the city's venerable barbershops.

BOOKSHOPS, BOOKBINDERS & PRINTERS

✦

BRATTLE BOOK SHOP

9 WEST STREET, BOSTON
☎ (617) 542-0210
🚋 MBTA RED OR GREEN LINE TO PARK STREET;
OR MBTA SILVER, ORANGE, OR RED LINE TO
DOWNTOWN CROSSING
MONDAY-SATURDAY 9AM TO 5:30PM

✦

*W*HEN GEORGE GLOSS BOUGHT THE BRATTLE
BOOK SHOP IN 1949 IT WAS A GAMBLE THAT
he could make a success of it. The Scollay Square
area where it was situated had become a magnet
for sailors in search of tattoo parlors, ladies of the
night, and burlesque venues. (The Old Howard and
the Casino were particularly renowned.) Although
earlier this area had been a center for bookstores
and book stalls, by the 1940s, Scollay Square hardly
appealed to bibliophiles.

The bookshop—founded in 1825 by Thomas M.
Burnham in the basement of the Old South Church
—had, with its surroundings, fallen on hard times.
That was why book-loving young George Gloss
thought he could afford it. So what is believed to be
the oldest continuously operated antiquarian bookstore in the nation became his to nurture. When, in
the 1960s, Scollay Square was demolished as part

of an ambitious city development program that did away with its derelict alleys and lanes and replaced them with Brutalist City Hall and its surrounding Plaza, the nineteenth-century Sears Crescent Building in which Gloss had by then set up shop, though preserved, was taken by eminent domain. The bookseller eventually established himself on West Street.

The cozy, five-story nineteenth-century townhouse into which he moved in 1969 seemed tailor-made for a bookshop until the night eleven years later when it burned to the ground. But for the determination of Gloss, his son, Ken (today's owner), and the assistance of book-loving friends, the Brattle Book Shop might have gone out of existence. But devoted customers, including then-Mayor Kevin White, whose mother had long frequented the bookstore, arrived with cartons of books for it to sell. Estate owners who had been putting off relinquishing their old book collections invited him to buy them so he could fill his shop again. The Brattle Book Shop was back in business.

Today its inventory of 150,000 to 200,000 books —first editions, works with fine leather bindings, autographs—occupies three floors of a fireproof red-brick building next door to the old store. In the empty lot where the old store once stood, outdoor bookshelves attract browsers all day long.

THE HARCOURT BINDERY, INC.

51 MELCHER STREET, BOSTON
☎ (617) 542-5858
🚇 MBTA RED LINE TO SOUTH STATION
MONDAY-FRIDAY 7:30AM TO 4PM

✦

A LEATHER SLIPCASE TO PROTECT CHARLES
DICKENS'S SLEEPING CAP AND ANOTHER FOR
the stolen door key to the honeymoon suite of the
Duke and Duchess of Windsor are among the custom-made items this bindery, begun in 1900, has
produced. It has also done binding for the Vatican
Library and for the First Church of Christ Scientist's
pulpit edition of Mary Baker Eddy's *Science and
Health With Key to the Scriptures.*

In its early years, when it was Huegle, Quinby
and Co., Harcourt Bindery (so named later for the
street near Copley Place where it long stood) was
involved in a scam. Its then-owner, Frederick J.
Quinby, was accused of failing to supply all the elegant leather- and silk-bound sets of the classics—
then much in demand with wealthy widows—that
had been ordered and paid for by customers.

The scandal hurt business, but the crisis passed
after the firm was bought, in 1911, by three well-to-
do art patrons, Gilmer Clapp and Oakes and William

H. Ames. It not only survived, but flourished. As this was the heyday of the Arts and Crafts movement in Boston, with its emphasis on the decorative arts, bookbinding was much admired.

From the beginning, fine leather hand binding was the specialty of the Harcourt Bindery. Handsome leather-bound Harcourt volumes filled the bookshelves of Hollywood actors and actresses in the days after World War I, remembers Fred Young, who worked at the bindery from 1917 to 1971 and co-owned it with Walter F. Johnston between 1931 and 1969.

In 1971, after his partner's death, Young sold the business, still on Harcourt Street, to one of his employees, Samuel Ellenport, a former Brown University history instructor, and his wife, Emily, who are its present owners.

In 1986, the Ellenports moved the bindery from Harcourt Street to its present location among print shops and printing equipment suppliers not far from the city's old leather district near South Station. Today, the owners and their ten employees not only bind for libraries and book dealers but also for private booklovers who may want their childhood copy of Beatrix Potter's *The Tale of Peter Rabbit* restored to pass on to their grandchildren; or they may wish to preserve their own grandmother's *The*

Boston Cooking School Cook Book, edited by Fannie Merritt Farmer, with generations of notes scrawled on its pages.

A visit to the fourth-floor bindery is replete with the rich scents of leather and glue. Sam Ellenport's office is lined with wainscoting preserved from the Harcourt Street bindery and furnished with the old bindery's big black safe, roll-top desk, and 1903 time clock. Some of the limited edition volumes the firm binds and sells are displayed on shelves. Prices range from $200 for a leather-bound Heritage Press classic to $2,500 for a *Diary of Anne Frank* illustrated with twelve original watercolors. A new leather binding for an old book may cost $200 to $500, a cloth binding $50 to $75. The company also custom designs wedding albums, jewelry boxes, picture frames, and stationery portfolios for the discerning buyer who is welcome to visit during business hours.

SCHELL PRINTING COMPANY

3399 WASHINGTON STREET, JAMAICA PLAIN
☎ (617) 524-3800
🚋 MBTA ORANGE LINE TO GREEN STREET
MONDAY-FRIDAY 8:30AM TO 5PM;
SATURDAY 9AM TO 1PM

✦

*A*T THE SCHELL PRINTING COMPANY, THE MACHINE FOR TURNING ROUND CORNERS into square ones that John M. Schell used more than a century ago is still in use. And Schell's great grandsons, Bill and Andy, display in old type cases the wooden letters used in the early days of printing.

Just back from the Spanish American War, where he served in the Navy, John Schell opened a small printing company in Scollay Square in downtown Boston in 1892. In time, his sons Eddie and Al took over, and in the 1930s heyday of four-time Boston Mayor James Michael Curley, it was the Schell Printing Company that produced his election cards. One of these still hangs on the wall of the little company's front office alongside a vintage postcard of Curley. Also displayed on the office wall is a company-printed poster announcing a performance by Eddie Schell and his Boston Jazz Band, which played clubs all over the city in the 1920s and 1930s.

When, as part of urban renewal, demolition of Scollay Square began in the late 1950s, Schell's moved to Eggleston Square in Jamaica Plain until a fire demolished the building in which it was located. Since 1965, Schell's has been on Washington Street, still printing business cards, wedding invitations, letterhead stationery, and small books as it has always done. In the two-room shop, in addition to the memorabilia that covers the walls, visitors can hear and see two Heidelberg letterpresses, a digital printer, and an offset press at work.

SCHOENHOF'S FOREIGN BOOKS

76 A MOUNT AUBURN STREET, CAMBRIDGE
☎ (617) 547-8855
🚆 MBTA RED LINE TO HARVARD SQUARE
MONDAY-SATURDAY 10AM TO 6PM;
THURSDAY TO 8PM

✦

*N*EAR HARVARD SQUARE IN THE HEART OF CAMBRIDGE IS A STORE THAT HOLDS A unique place in bookstore history: It has the largest selection of foreign language books in North America, with books of literature in twenty to thirty languages and books and materials in the language learning section in 700 to 800 tongues. (These include Basque, Old Icelandic, Occcitan, and Tetum, a language of the Pacific islands.) As a result, Schoenhof's is renowned among academics and language lovers, drawing visitors from far corners of the world. On display in the main part of the two-section 2,500-square foot basement store is one copy of every title in its inventory of some 60,000 titles.

Not much is known about its first owner, Carl Schoenhof. The store logo says it opened in 1856, but the enterprise may have fallen on hard times, for eleven years later, the Boston City Directory describes Schoenhof as working as a mere clerk in the Tremont Street foreign bookstore DeVries, Ibarra & Co.

In 1871, Schoenhof again had a book supply business, this time called Schoenhof and Moeller. His partner was a woman, Fannie Moeller, although it was rare, indeed, to have a woman business partner in nineteenth century New England.

That partnership did not last long, but Carl Schoenhof's love of books was apparently unflagging. He moved his bookstore from street to street in downtown Boston until his death in 1911. Much of his clientele was from the immigrant German community in the city, and so German language books were an original emphasis. His successors kept the store in downtown Boston until the 1930s, when New York's Librairie Française bought it and Bill Tutin, an antiquarian bookdealer representing that firm, moved it to Massachusetts Avenue in downtown Cambridge, in close proximity to Harvard Square. There, in the 1940s, Paul Mueller, a former Austrian bookseller, became its famed manager.

It was he who turned the store into the comprehensive foreign language bookstore it is today. Mueller's own bookstore in Vienna had been closed down by the Nazis, and he had spent eight months in Büchenwald before managing to get to New York. There he worked as a butler before moving to

Cambridge. He and his wife, Greta, in time, would become Schoenhof's part owners.

During the Second World War, it was the major distributor of German literature outside of Germany. When the United States government, as part of its de-Nazification program for prisoners of war, wanted to know what prisoners should read, they asked Mueller. He sold them the books he recommended, and the federal government became one of the store's largest accounts. The company also became a small-scale publisher of German books by immigrant writers.

After Mueller's death in 1964, his wife and employees managed it for several years. Then, in 1981, the French publisher, Editions Gallimard, became its owner. The store went from being a small family-run business to one with larger ambitions. French became a specialty, with the works of Zola, Flaubert, Rimbaud, and others; French literature retains a key place in the store's inventory today. In fact, author John Dos Passos, writing of Schoenhof's in its days under Mueller, remarked on how the store was a good, cheap source of French books. In 1984, Schoenhof's moved a street away to Harvard's Spee Club building—slightly off the beaten track, but still easily found by book lovers.

There have been many book-loving customers over the years, including Henry David Thoreau, Ralph Waldo Emerson, Albert Einstein, Carlos Fuentes, Henry Kissinger, Edmund Wilson, and John Updike.

There is nothing fusty or musty about today's Schoenhof's. Along with its 60,000 titles, largely classics, its language-learning books, CDs, and tapes, there are children's books in many languages, and a multilingual staff to help customers find them. Since 2005, the store's owners have been MEP/Distribooks of Chicago.

In Brief

ACME BOOKBINDING, 100 CAMBRIDGE STREET, CHARLESTOWN. J.G. Roberts began binding books on Water Street in Boston in 1821. Acme Bookbinding is notable for having bound Harriet Beecher Stowe's *Uncle Tom's Cabin*, or *Life Among the Lowly*, in 1852. The bindery has been bought and sold several times throughout the years, and is currently owned by the Paul Parisi family. Acme binds books for publishers, colleges, universities, libraries, and individuals, and claims to be the oldest continuously operating bookbindery in the world.

CLOTHING &
GENERAL STORES

✦

E. A. DAVIS

579 WASHINGTON STREET, WELLESLEY
☎ (781) 235-0688
🚆 COMMUTER RAIL FROM SOUTH STATION
TO WELLESLEY
MONDAY-SATURDAY 9:30AM TO 6PM;
SUNDAY NOON TO 5PM

✦

*W*HEN THERE WAS SNOW ON THE GROUND OUTSIDE AND A CRACKLING FIRE IN THE BIG stone fireplace at Emma A. Davis' dry goods store in 1904, there were few cozier places to shop in all of Wellesley. You could, of course, buy gentlemen's furnishings and sporting goods at the town's men's store or a hat at the milliner's (where mourning goods were also available). You could have tea at the Wellesley Inn on Washington Street, before hiring a conveyance to take you home from the hack and livery stable. But there was always something special about E.A. Davis's.

On shelves lining the walls were bolts of all the fabric anyone could want, as well as glass drawers of ribbons and buttons. Foundations and hats were also sold. Wellesley, with its college for serious young women who were certain to need thread and needles and such during the school year, was a logical place for a dry goods store.

The store prospered to such an extent that Emma's brother, Charles E. Holman, who was in the same business in Allston, felt she should have a bigger and better location than the Shattuck Building where her store was first situated. And so, after World War I, he built the sturdy granite Holman Block on Washington Street to house E.A. Davis and a handful of other small retail businesses. In the 1920s, his son, Clarence, took over the store, expanding it considerably. Although it still filled sewing needs, it came to resemble a modern department store with furniture and lamps sold in the basement and toys on the balcony. It was always notable for the shiny little overhead trolleys that carried the money to and from the cashier's desk.

In 1975, following the death of Clarence Holman, Robert L. Skolnick, who had been in the menswear business in Wellesley, became the owner. Today's E.A. Davis, run by Skolnick's son, Rob, still has many of the earmarks of its past. A number of its clerks have been with the company for decades. Vintage oak display cabinets continue to show off its wares. Its two hand-cranked cash registers, though no longer in use, hark back to 1912. As always, shoppers can find needles and thread and safety pins, but Lilly Pulitzer sportswear has replaced toys on the balcony. Racks of pastel Lacoste blouses and shirts are found where corset stays were sold in the 1950s. Though there is no longer the stone fireplace of Emma Davis's day, the store that still bears her name continues to accommodate third and fourth generations of discerning customers.

FILENE'S BASEMENT

426 WASHINGTON STREET AT DOWNTOWN
CROSSING, BOSTON
☎ (617) 348-7848
🚆 MBTA ORANGE OR RED LINE TO
DOWNTOWN CROSSING
MONDAY-FRIDAY 9:30AM TO 8PM; SATURDAY 9AM
TO 8PM; SUNDAY 11AM TO 7PM

+

YEAR AFTER YEAR, FILENE'S BASEMENT, FOUNDED IN 1909, IS LISTED—AFTER FANEUIL Hall—as Boston's top "free" tourist attraction. Some 10,000 to 15,000 shoppers pass annually through its doors. They gleefully leave with designer coats, suits, and dresses bought at half or even one-quarter of the original price or with low-priced household goods of the highest quality.

Wilhelm Katz, a German immigrant, thought to anglicize his name from the German for "cat" to the English "feline," but a mistake was made at Immigration and it was misspelled "Filene." From 1849 on, William had been, variously, a Boston tailor and the owner of shops selling trimmings, lace, veils, and gloves in Boston, Salem, and Lynn. Finally he founded William Filene & Sons on Washington Street in 1890, turning it over that same year to his two sons, Edward and Lincoln. It was Edward, in the basement of the women's ready-to-wear store, who, after his father's death, began the store's well-known practice of automatically marking down items that were slow to sell upstairs.

According to Edward's plan, the store agreed to pay immediate cash to manufacturers to rid them of unsold stock. Then, if the upstairs store had not sold an item in fourteen days, it would go to the tunnel basement (so named because the entrance was through a tunnel from the subway), where its price was reduced 25 percent. If it was still on hand after twenty-one selling days, the price was cut to 50 percent; after twenty-eight days, the markdown was 75 percent, and if the article had not sold in thirty-five days, it was given to charity. Today, the markdown system continues to be automatic, though it takes slightly longer for the big reductions to take place. In the beginning, it was only Filene's own merchandise that was part of this system, but soon other manufacturers and retailers asked to be part of the mix, including international couturiers and major department stores such as Bloomingdale's, Bergdorf Goodman, Neiman Marcus, and Saks Fifth Avenue.

In 2006, after 118 years as one of Boston's leading department stores, William Filene & Sons was bought by Federated Department Stores, owners of

R.H. Macy. Filene's Basement, however, already a separate entity, had been bought six years earlier by Retail Ventures of Columbus, Ohio. And so, where it has been since the beginning, underneath the old store, in the pedestrian shopping district that is Downtown Crossing, Filene's Basement continues selling, as it always has, items at reduced prices. A second Filene's Basement, however—this one above ground with a bright and airy contemporary look— has also opened at 497 Boylston Street in the stylish Copley Square area.

THE HARVARD COOP

1400 MASSACHUSETTS AVENUE, CAMBRIDGE

☎ (617) 499-2000

🚆 MBTA RED LINE TO HARVARD SQUARE

MONDAY-SATURDAY 9AM TO 10PM;

SUNDAY 10AM TO 9PM

✦

ONE FEBRUARY DAY IN 1882, HARVARD JUNIOR CHARLES HAYDEN KIP INVITED FORTY-TWO fellow students to his room in Holworthy Hall. Harvard Square merchants were overcharging for books, for the firewood that heated dormitory rooms, and for other student necessities, Kip felt. He proposed forming a cooperative society to which members would pay minimal membership fees and in return be allowed to buy, at reduced prices, from a store that their contributions would help support.

A month later, the Harvard Cooperative Society opened at 13 College Row on Massachusetts Avenue. The items it had to sell filled only a few five-foot shelves in what was basically a fruit store. Those making purchases had paid $2 annual dues. The store moved several times that year, but the society was a success. By 1883, it had 699 student and fourteen faculty members.

In the first few years of its operation, however,

it didn't always do well. To increase business, membership fees were reduced to $1.50, then $1. In 1887 it was decided that anyone connected with any part of the college, including Radcliffe and the Episcopal Seminary, would be allowed to shop there, whether they belonged to the Coop or not. Prices for everything except books were increased to be more in line with those that the regular merchants were charging in the Square.

In time, buying at the society store—though not membership in the society—was open to anyone, with or without a university affiliation. In 1917, when Massachusetts Institute of Technology moved to Cambridge, MIT students were allowed to become members of the Harvard Coop and to share in the dividends.

Today's red-brick Harvard Coop (always known as the "Coop," as in chicken coop), was constructed in 1925; in 1927 a branch was opened at Harvard Business School, and in 1937 a Coop was built on Massachusetts Avenue at MIT. By the 1960s, the Coop, selling clothes as well as books, stationery, and supplies, was the largest department store in the Harvard Square area.

In 1967, still another Coop—this one at Children's Hospital Medical Center at the corner of Longwood and Brookline Avenues in Boston—was opened. It attracts members from the teaching hospitals connected with Harvard and from such other neighboring colleges as Simmons and Wheelock.

Today there are six Coops, but the largest is the Harvard Square original with its six-story general readership bookstore facing the square. An annex across Palmer Street carries textbooks, stationery, and Harvard-related clothing. As it has been since the days when students were buying their own firewood, Coop members are eligible for the annual patronage rebate that makes purchases affordable.

KEEZER'S

140 RIVER STREET, CAMBRIDGE
☎ (617) 547-2455
🚇 MBTA RED LINE TO CENTRAL SQUARE
MONDAY-SATURDAY 10AM TO 6PM

✦

LEGEND HAS IT THAT IN THEIR HARVARD DAYS, BOTH TEDDY ROOSEVELT AND FDR DROPPED by Keezer's at the end of each school year. There, at the used clothing store, they would exchange their fine, custom-made suits for ready cash when they were short of funds. Another future president, when he, too, was a Harvard undergraduate, reportedly sent his valet to Keezer's each spring to sell cast-off clothing—John F. Kennedy.

Max Keezer, a Dutch immigrant, opened his first used clothing store on Massachusetts Avenue in 1895. He would go out onto the street and engage Harvardians who passed by, promising them "top dollar" for their tailor-made coats and suits. Then he would offer the second-hand garments to less well-off students. Working along with Max were his brothers, Joe and Luke. Fred Salo, who had been a partner with the last of the brothers, Joe, took over in the mid-1960s after Joe's death. He kept the store until 1978, when he sold it and its entire stock of

[51]

vintage clothing to Len Goldstein.

Only six months later, virtually everything that Fred Salo had kept in the cellar turned out to be just what the producers of the movie *The Brinks Job* were looking for. "There were *Guys and Dolls* suits and gabardine raincoats—all that kind of vintage stuff," Goldstein recalls. In 1987, when *The Witches of Eastwick* was being made, Keezer's stock was wiped out again by the costume designers. And for many years, when Harvard's *Hasty Pudding Show* was being produced in the spring, Keezer's was a principal source of its costumes.

In 1985, Goldstein moved the store to Central Square to a circa-1910 theater that had been converted into commercial space, where it remains today. In the days of Max Keezer, this neighborhood was home to laborers who worked in the clay pits of nearby Fresh Pond; today, Central Square is home to many graduate students.

In Keezer's warehouse-like interior, customers sort through some 2,000 suits (including Italian designer brands), 2,500 shirts, and 4,000 to 5,000 new and used tuxedos. There are ties and cummerbunds, top hats, Mad Hatter hats, Chesterfield coats, English handmade shoes, and pumps that—to all appearances—have danced at only a single dance.

Young and old customers, distinguished professors and scholarship students, can be seen most days thumbing through the racks in search of just the right suit or tie for a special occasion. Tuxedos may be either bought or rented. Until a few years ago, one of Keezer's oldest patrons, a member of the Harvard class of 1913, brought in his sons and grandsons so they, too, could be outfitted at Keezer's.

MORGAN MEMORIAL GOODWILL INDUSTRIES, INC.

1010 HARRISON AVENUE, BOSTON

☎ (617) 445-1010

🚇 MBTA ORANGE LINE TO RUGGLES AND ANY
BUS FROM THERE TO DUDLEY STATION; OR
SILVER LINE TO MELNEA CASS BOULEVARD

MONDAY-SATURDAY 9AM TO 6PM;

SUNDAY NOON TO 6PM

✦

*T*HE REVEREND EDGAR HELMS, A YOUNG
METHODIST MINISTER FROM IOWA WHO HAD
just been graduated, in 1893, from the Boston University Divinity School, suffered a serious disappointment. He wanted to be an overseas missionary but had been assigned to the Morgan Chapel in Boston's South End. The area, like the Back Bay, had been created from "made land," planned to become a stylish area with broad, shaded streets and small parks. But once fashionable Back Bay came into being, these grand plans were forgotten, and the South End became home to great-house servants and the immigrant poor.

The Rev. Helms made the best of his assignment. Soon he was soliciting funds for those in need from the wealthy residents of Beacon Hill and the

Back Bay. When, in the early years of the twentieth century, the city's wealthy were also feeling hard pressed and declined his requests for funds, he asked them for contributions of old clothes instead.

With a burlap bag slung over his shoulder, Helms went door-to-door collecting items for the needy of the South End. But what he collected was not simply given away. To develop a work ethic among those he was helping, he gave his bounty to the poor to sort, mend, and clean, put the items on sale, and then paid the workers from the proceeds. The first Morgan Memorial store was established on Shawmut Avenue; additional stores were opened later throughout the city.

Today, in this 14,000-square-foot store built in 1986, donated clothing, jewelry, household goods, furniture, and art are processed and sold, not only to residents of the area, but also to bargain- and treasure-hunters from all parts of the city and all walks of life. A smaller store is located at 470 West Broadway in the South End.

ZIMMAN'S INC.

80 MARKET STREET, LYNN
☎ (781) 598-9432
🚊 COMMUTER RAIL FROM NORTH STATION
MONDAY-SATURDAY 9:30AM TO 5:30PM;
THURSDAY TO 8:30PM

✦

*I*N THE EARLY TWENTIETH CENTURY, LYNN AND WEST LYNN WERE BUSTLING INDUSTRIAL cities twelve miles north of Boston. General Electric had a large factory in West Lynn, and shoe manufacturing thrived in both Lynns. Young immigrant men arrived in large numbers to fill the factory jobs; they lived in boarding houses and spoke little or no English. As they saved money, they would bring their families from the old country to the new. Today, after having gone through a period of economic and social downturn (during which a popular jingle began "Lynn, Lynn, city of sin"), Lynn is undergoing a rejuvenation. Zimman's—which stayed put during Lynn's time of adversity—remains a stylish oasis.

In 1909, Lithuanian-born Morris Zimman, who spoke Russian and German as well as his native language, opened a store on Summer Street in West Lynn selling household goods to the newly arrived families. He made sure to offer fabric since the immigrant women were in the habit of making their own and their children's clothes. Morris Zimman's four sons all helped out in their father's store.

Zimman's son Barry came home from the Navy after World War II to join his father in the store, but by then the business seemed old-fashioned to him. Barry wanted to open a more up-to-date store, so in 1947 he bought the 1903 Goddard Brothers Department Store building and opened a general merchandise store like the one that his father had in West Lynn, except that his was self-service. He called his store Zimman's, too. Morris said the self-service concept would never work—that customers needed a salesperson's advice and help to make purchases—but in 1966 he joined his son on Market Street anyway. Until 1990, Zimman's continued to be a self-service general merchandise store, eventually carrying only fabric since that seemed to hold the greatest appeal to customers. Sixteen years later, however, since their fabric salesroom only occupied the first floor of the old department store, Barry and his son Michael, who had come into the business, decided to fill the empty floors above with home furnishings.

Today, in the building with the tin-ceiling, rosewood walls, and mahogany staircase that once were the hallmarks of the original elegant Goddard

Brothers, Barry and Michael Zimman run what is the largest fabric store in the Boston area. The store displays bolts of shimmering silks and brocades, Provençal and Marimekko fabrics, in tiers from floor to ceiling, mostly for upholstery and draperies. On the second and third floors, furniture, lamps, and rugs are sold.

In Brief

JAMES F. FISKE'S GENERAL STORE, 776 WASHINGTON STREET, HOLLISTON. In 1876, James Fiske advertised that he was selling "Hats, Caps and Trunks, Railway and Steamship Tickets, Men's and Gent's Furnishings." Today, Fiske's owner, Louis Paltrineri—the fourth owner in the company's history—sells toys, games, crafts supplies, paper, books, balloons, penny candy, and more in his turn-of-the-century general store with its tin ceiling.

FLORISTS &
GARDEN CENTERS

✦

HOLBROW'S FLOWERS
BOSTON, INC.

100 CITY HALL PLAZA, BOSTON
☎ (617) 227-8057
🚇 MBTA GREEN LINE TO GOVERNMENT CENTER
MONDAY-FRIDAY 8:30AM TO 5PM;
SATURDAY 10AM TO NOON

✦

*I*N BARREN CITY HALL PLAZA, THE GIANT COP-
PER TEAKETTLE HANGING FROM AN UPPER
story on the corner of the Sears Crescent Building
is a unique delight. The 227 plus-gallon kettle was
cast in 1874 by the now defunct Oriental Tea Company as a successful advertising gimmick: When the
company promised forty pounds of tea to whomever
could accurately guess how much the kettle would
hold, thousands of contestants showed up.

That kettle and the curving red-brick nineteenth-
century building from which it hangs—which also
houses Holbrow's Flowers—are the sole survivors
from the time before the 1960s urban renewal project that created Boston's Government Center. For the
last eighteen years, Patricia Holbrow Long, a fourth-
generation florist, has been selling everything from
birds of paradise and ginger to roses and camellias.

In the 1890s her London-born great-grandfather, Frederick Willmore Holbrow, had greenhouses constructed beside his house in Dorchester. By 1896, he had grown enough to open F.W. Holbrow & Sons Flowers on that property. When his son Willmore Frederick took over the business after his father's death, he began selling flowers at the Boston Flower Exchange as well. Snapdragons, chrysanthemums, and camellias, in particular, were his specialties and, in time, he came to be known as Boston's Camellia King.

During World War II, Willmore Frederick Holbrow conceived the idea of sending flowers across the Atlantic. A serviceman stationed overseas who wished to send a bouquet to a wife or fiancée or mother on a special day could arrange to do it. Similarly, for those whose loved ones had been killed in action and were buried in a foreign cemetery, he helped devise a system to have flowers sent to decorate the graves. That system, still in operation, is called Interflora.

In 1949, W.F. Holbrow opened a shop on Province Street, but then moved several times. For a number of years, Holbrow's was on the ground floor of the Parker House. When she was fourteen, his granddaughter, Patricia, began working for him on school vacations and is now the owner of the busy little shop.

OLYMPIA FLOWER STORE, INC.

1745 WASHINGTON STREET, BOSTON

☎ (617) 262-2000

🚌 MBTA SILVER LINE TO NEWTON STREET

MONDAY-FRIDAY 9:00AM TO 6:30PM; SATURDAY
9:30AM TO 6:30PM; SUNDAY 10:30AM TO 3:30PM

✦

*W*HEN RUSSIAN IMMIGRANT LOUIS BORN-STEIN DECIDED TO OPEN A FLORIST SHOP IN the South End in 1903, the area was no longer the fashionable part of the city it once had been. The proper Bostonians were leaving, Irish immigrants were moving in, and the elevated train rumbled overhead. But the area boasted broad streets, parks, comfortable homes, and Boston Latin School and Roman Catholic Boston College. Across from the florist shop the English Gothic Cathedral of the Holy Cross soared, and still soars. When it was built in 1875, it was the largest Catholic church in New England.

Boston City Hospital was also close by, so Olympia began creating floral arrangements for hospital patients. Bornstein also came up with the idea of pre-packaging flowers for supermarkets in the city.

Olympia thrived in this mixed, colorful neighborhood where smalltime gangsters sometimes hung out at Mugar's Armenian Restaurant next door (Middle Easterners lived in the area, too). Boston Mayor James Michael Curley, "the poor man's friend," was a regular customer of Bornstein's, stopping in for bouquets for his wife, Mame. Olympia developed a loyal clientele among the neighborhood's old-time residents—Armenian, Syrian, Jewish, and Irish—but by the 1960s they began to move elsewhere. Olympia stayed in business, however, thanks to customers who kept buying from them even after settling in other parts of the city.

Today Louis's grandsons, Larry and Joe Bornstein, who have another shop in Brookline, own the flower shop. Olympia still makes arrangements for hospital patients, as it did in Louis' day, but it has expanded beyond individual to corporate customers, providing flowers for banks and businesses. Still, it hasn't forgotten its past. On the walls of the sprawling shop are photographs of the South End in the days of the El, the Minot Dance Hall, and the Puritan Movie Theater. Some photos date back more than a century.

RUSSELL'S GARDEN CENTER

397 BOSTON POST ROAD (ROUTE 20), WAYLAND
☎ (508) 358-2283
🚘 BY CAR, MASS TURNPIKE TO ROUTE 128 NORTH;
EXIT 26 TO ROUTE 20 WEST. THE FARM IS A LITTLE
MORE THAN FIVE MILES DOWN ROUTE 20.
DAILY 9AM-6PM AND UNTIL 8PM IN SPRING
AND IN DECEMBER

✦

I N 1876, AT THE AGE OF TWENTY-TWO, YOUNG SAMUEL RUSSELL OPENED "SAMUEL RUSSELL Provisions" in the center of Wayland to sell the meat and produce raised on his family farm. He went into the wholesale vegetable business as well, delivering farm produce by horse and wagon in neighboring areas.

In the next generation, his son Waldo, his horse-drawn wagon laden with produce, would make a seven-hour one-way trip from the farm to Boston's Faneuil Hall Market to sell eggs and vegetables. In 1920, Samuel Russell bought a Mack truck; after that his son was able to make the journey to Boston in only one hour.

But Waldo and his brother, Lewis, were not alone in having motorized vehicles. Cars had become popular and were being driven to the country on outings. To appeal to these new automobile owners, the brothers opened a roadside stand at the farm in 1925. To catch the eyes of drivers, they displayed the colorful cut flowers—gladiolas, delphiniums, asters, and zinnias—they had begun to grow.

For a while they continued selling wholesale at both Faneuil Hall and the Boston Flower Exchange, but the retail business at their farm stand was so profitable that they gradually ended their wholesale business.

Now, grown out of the produce market that began with his grandfather's provision store more than a century ago, Harvard-educated Lewis Russell Jr., along with his wife, daughter, and son-in-law, have a nursery, flower store, garden supply shop, gift shop, and display gardens where they invite visitors to stroll. In addition, one day a week, in season, local farmers hold a market on the grounds.

FOOD & SPIRITS SHOPS

✦

BENT'S COOKIE FACTORY

7 PLEASANT STREET, MILTON

☎ (617) 698-5945

🚋 MBTA RED LINE TO ASHMONT AND
TROLLEY FROM ASHMONT TO CENTRAL
AVENUE, MILTON; OR MBTA BUS FROM
ASHMONT TO RANDOLPH AVENUE, MILTON
MONDAY-FRIDAY 7AM TO 5PM;
SATURDAY 7:30AM TO 3PM

✦

IN 1801, THERE WAS A CLEAR WATER SPRING NEAR HIGHLAND STREET AND A GRISTMILL ON the Neponset River Falls in Milton. Thirty-year-old Josiah Bent, a local farmer, made good use of both, creating the water biscuits he sold as provisions for ship's crews. Known eventually as Bent's Cold Water Crackers, there were made simply of a mixture of flour and cold water and rolled out and baked in a 500-degree oven. Bent's biscuits would last indefinitely as long as they were kept dry.

The story goes that whenever his flour and water biscuits were cooling after being taken out of the 500-degree oven, they crackled, and, on one occasion, Bent asked to be brought some of those "crackers." And so it is that he is credited with having introduced a new word into the American lexicon.

Bent kept Bent and Company until 1830 when, nearing sixty, he sold it to his son, Samuel Tucker Bent, and his son-in-law, Deacon Samuel Adams. Young Bent soon left to go West, perhaps to sell the crackers to cousins who had established a trading fort on the frontier.

Back home in Milton, Deacon Adams expanded the bakery. When the Civil War began, Bent and Company was called upon to make hardtack for the Union Army. The recipe was the same as for the biscuits, except the dough was more thinly rolled, layered, cut into three and one-eighth-inch squares, and pricked with sixteen holes to allow the steam to escape. Legend has it that frontiersman Kit Carson, who had married into the family of the Western Bents, carried Bent's biscuits on his journeys.

With the death of Deacon Adams, the company was split in two. Bent and Company went to the deacon's heirs and was eventually bought by the National Biscuit Company, which briefly operated it until closing it in the 1920s.

The other branch, founded in 1884 by Samuel Bent's son—the G.H. Bent Company—did a brisk business not only in crackers but in baked beans and brown bread as well. At the end of a week of baking crackers in a hot, hot oven, the wood fire would be cooled down for the weekend, making the temperature just right for the slow cooking of succulent Boston baked beans. These were then carried by horse and wagon and sold door to door.

G.H. Bent Company passed through several hands before it was sold, in 1943, to Arthur S. Pierrotti, who had come as a boy from Italy to Boston's North End, then the center of Boston's Italian community. Cafes, restaurants, and pastry shops—all with Italian names—lined Hanover Street. Edging Salem Street were butcher shops, fish markets, and greengrocers. On narrow side streets, outside the four- and five-story dwellings, housewives with southern Italian accents energetically discussed what they would put on their dinner tables.

Pierrotti had been making ginger ale until World War II, when a shortage of sugar for the drink and cork for the bottle tops forced him out of business. When he saw a newspaper ad for the cracker company, it appealed to him, although he knew nothing about baking, and he bought it. Today, Pierrotti's son Gene runs the bakery in the same clapboard-sided building that G.H. Bent built for his fledgling business in 1892. On its walls hang pictures of the baked bean and brown bread delivery wagons of the company's past and labels from Bent's Cold Water Crackers.

In his boyhood, Gene Pierrotti would go into

the Milton woods regularly to collect bundles of hardwood to fire the 12-foot Dutch ovens his father inherited when he bought the store. Today, the ovens are gas-fired, but the crackers and beans are the same as they have always been. In addition, sandwiches are now sold.

The company's name was changed to Bent's Cookie Factory when the bakery began selling cookies, in addition to crackers, to the United States Navy in World War II.

BOSCHETTO'S BAKERY

4172 WASHINGTON STREET, ROSLINDALE

☎ (617) 323-5702

🚇 MBTA ORANGE LINE TO FOREST HILLS AND
MBTA BUS #34-35-36 TO ROSLINDALE VILLAGE

MONDAY-SATURDAY 7AM TO 7PM;
SUNDAY 7AM TO 5:30PM

✦

DEVOTEES OF *PANE DI SCALA*—LADDER-SHAPED SICILIAN BREAD—AND ROUND, CRUSTY *ROTONDA* come from all over Boston to buy them from Boschetto's Bakery, as they have for generations.

The Boschetto patriarch, Andrew Sr., arrived from southern Italy in the 1880s and learned to bake by apprenticing. He soon opened his own bread bakery on Salem Street in Boston's North End. Before long, customers on the South Shore and even Maine were asking for deliveries to their front doors, and Andrew Boschetto was sending bread trucks out to them, as much as 100 miles away. The original Boschetto's still exists (see p. 88) but is no longer in family hands.

In 1952, three of Andrew Sr.'s sons, Larry, Andy, and John, opened a new version of the old bakery in Roslindale and expanded beyond bread. Pink and green Italian butter cookies, flaky Neapolitans, rum cakes, and cat pies—made from the cut-off edges of cake mixed with sliced apples and spices and refrigerated before being cut into squares—are now sold.

Andy and John, both in their seventies, are still baking, but they sold the bakery to Joseph Murphy, a much younger entrepreneur who moved from the corporate world to the world of baked goods some years ago.

V. CIRACE & SON, INC.

173 NORTH STREET, BOSTON

☎ (617) 227-3193

🚊 MBTA ORANGE LINE TO HAYMARKET

MONDAY-THURSDAY 9AM TO 7PM;

FRIDAY, SATURDAY 9AM TO 8PM

✦

*W*HEN VINCENZA AND ERNESTO CIRACE OPENED THEIR WHOLESALE GROCERY, tobacco,and sundries shop here at the corner of North and Richmond Streets in 1906, the North End was the center of Boston's Italian colony. It was also one of the most historic areas of the city. Only a block away is Paul Revere's frame house, the oldest house that still stands on its original site in Boston. Where the Ciraces settled, the Red Lyon Inn had welcomed guests in Colonial times, while just a short walk away is the Old North Church in which the lanterns were hung that sent Revere on his famous midnight ride.

In the next century, Irish immigrants moved to the area, then Jewish merchants from Eastern Europe, and finally the Italians whose presence made the Ciraces from Salerno feel at home.

Vincenza and Ernesto Cirace ran their store together, beginning a tradition of women in the family business that has continued into the third generation. Today, their grandchildren, Jeffrey and Lisa Lynne Cirace, own and operate the concern.

But it is a vastly different store from the one of 1906. Then it didn't seem appropriate to sell liquor. But when the Cirace children, Eda and Ernest, entered the business, they prevailed upon their elders to add beer, wine, and spirits to their merchandise, and Circace's became the second store in Boston to be licensed to sell liquor after Prohibition ended. For forty years it sold tobacco and groceries as well. Then in 1953, a wholesale liquor business was added to the already prospering retail operation. Today, the groceries are gone, and Cirace's shelves are dominated by fine Italian wines (as well as other wines and spirits). Colorful Italian ceramics, grappa glasses, pasta, biscotti, chocolates, and fine cigars are also sold, and gift baskets are made to order for the holidays.

DELUCA'S MARKET

11 CHARLES STREET, BOSTON
☎ (617) 523-4343
🚇 MBTA RED LINE TO MGH OR PARK
MONDAY–SATURDAY 7AM TO 10PM;
SUNDAY 7AM TO 9PM

✦

*A*T THE FOOT OF FASHIONABLE BEACON HILL—
SITE OF EARLY NINETEENTH-CENTURY
red-brick townhouses and quaint alleys—sedate
Louisburg Square stands above Charles Street. It is
to Charles Street that residents of the Hill tend to go
for everyday shopping.

Once it was home to such literary folk as Oliver
Wendell Holmes, Sarah Orne Jewett, and James T.
Fields, co-founder of *The Atlantic Monthly*, but today
it is a street that mixes tony antiques stores, cafes,
and art galleries with more mundane drugstores,
dry cleaners, and hardware stores. Here DeLuca's
Market had its beginnings in 1898 when the Giuffre
family opened a produce and grocery store.

In 1914, young Joseph DeLuca from Sicily got
a job as a stock boy there. In less than a decade he
was a partner in the store and its name had become
Giuffre and DeLuca. Then in 1924, Joseph became
the market's sole owner, renaming it DeLuca's. It

remained his until 1953 when his brother-in-law, Virgil Aiello, took over. Today, Virgil Jr. is its owner.

From floor to ceiling, DeLuca's is crammed with canned goods, jars, bottles, and packets. Their contents may be as mundane as peanut butter or as exotic as roasted garlic honey, white asparagus, or octopus. Colorful Italian ceramics crown the store's top shelves and decorate its walls.

A pungent fragrance emanates from the counter where hundreds of foreign and domestic cheeses are sold. Fine wines cram the shelves. De Luca's has its own butcher, and fresh fish is also available. Vegetables and fruits spill over the boxes in its produce section.

Virgil Aiello likes to boast how, in the days when John F. Kennedy was President of the United States, his cook continued to call DeLuca's for items that Kennedy needed for Hyannis Compound dinners.

MORSE FISH COMPANY

1401 WASHINGTON STREET, BOSTON
☎ 617-262-9375
🚊 MBTA SILVER LINE TO WEST DEDHAM STREET
MONDAY-THURSDAY 11AM-8PM; FRIDAY 11AM
TO 9PM; SATURDAY 11AM TO 8PM;
SUNDAY NOON TO 8PM

✦

*A*LL DAY LONG, THE TANTALIZING SMELL OF FRIED FISH EMANATES FROM THE MORSE Fish Company onto Washington Street. The fish market has been an institution of the South End since 1903. In those days, when the market sold wholesale as well as retail, it was located on Dover Street. Horses and wagons would haul the catches up from the docks, and fish would then be piled into wheelbarrows and taken inside to be readied for customers.

Daniel J. Morse was the market's founder and owner until the late 1930s, when Russell Huntley, a relative who was farming in Milton, decided to try his hand at running a fish market instead. In time, he bought his own boat and hired a crew. By then, Morse's had moved to Washington Street near East Berkeley. It still sold fish wholesale as well as retail, but cooked fish was not part of the business. Then in 1983, John Blacker, who had worked in the fish shop as a boy, became the owner. He gave up the wholesale operation, put in a few Formica tables, and began serving meals as well. The fish shop has been in its present location since 1963. In business with Blacker are his two sons and a partner, George Doherty.

Today, the mussels, clam strips, fish cakes, crab cakes, Cajun catfish, lobster and crab salad, and fish sandwiches are the larger part of the business. For those who still prefer to cook their fish at home, however, Morse's fish counter remains full of denizens of the deep.

NECCO

(New England Confectionery Company)

135 AMERICAN LEGION HIGHWAY, REVERE

☎ (781) 485-4500

🚇 MBTA BLUE LINE TO WONDERLAND

MONDAY-FRIDAY 8:30AM TO 5PM

✦

*H*AD IT NOT BEEN FOR THE TWO AND A HALF TONS OF NECCO WAFERS ANTARCTIC explorer Admiral Richard E. Byrd took to the South Pole in the 1930s to help sustain his men, his expedition might never have succeeded. And had it not been for Oliver R. Chase, a young English immigrant to Boston who in 1847 invented the lozenge cutter that was the first American candy machine, there would have been no NECCOs.

Delighted with what his machine could do, Oliver and his brother, Silas, opened Chase and Company on Congress Street and began producing paper-thin wafer candies of sugar, corn syrup, and gums in orange, lemon, lime, clove, chocolate, cinnamon, licorice, and wintergreen flavors. In the 1880s, Daniel, another brother, invented a machine that could print words on lozenges. This led to the company's producing heart-shaped wafers with loving sayings printed on them, Conversation Hearts.

In 1901, Chase and Company joined with two other New England candy companies—Fobes Hayward and Wright and Moody—to form the New England Confectionery Company. The new firm built its plant, the largest confectionery plant in the country at that time, at Summer and Melcher Streets.

They stayed there, acquiring other candy companies along the way, until 1947, when they moved to Cambridge. There, for decades, passersby along the Charles River enjoyed the sugary fragrance in the air and the depiction of a tasty pastel NECCO wafer on the factory's brick wall. After NECCO celebrated its 150th anniversary in 1996 and painted its water tower to resemble a package of NECCO wafers, the water tower became a Boston-Cambridge landmark.

In 2003, NECCO moved its plant to Revere, where, in a small candy shop, devotees of NECCO wafers and Conversation Hearts, molasses and peanut butter Mary Janes, Clark Bars, Sky Bars, Thin Mints, and Malted Milk Balls—all confections made today at NECCO—can find these favorite sweets.

WENHAM TEA HOUSE

4 MONUMENT STREET, WENHAM
☎ (978) 468-1235
🚃 COMMUTER RAIL FROM NORTH STATION
MONDAY TO SATURDAY, 9:30AM TO 5PM
TEA: 3:15 TO 4:30PM

✦

WITH THE WORDS: "TO ADORN AND MAKE MORE ATTRACTIVE THE TOWN OF WENHAM," a small group of women established the Wenham Village Improvement Society in 1893, allowing membership to any woman of good repute who subscribed to its constitution and bylaws and made an annual payment of fifty cents. The first act of the organization was to spend $8 for six chestnut, two maple, and two evergreen trees to beautify the town. Over time the society saw to the installation of street lights and street signs, cleaned up public areas, and provided funds for such summer programs as basket weaving and sewing.

It soon became clear, however, that a regular source of funds was necessary if these improvement projects were to continue. So in 1911 the society decided to purchase the old Hobbs Harness Shop beside the Congregational Church on Monument Square and transform it into a tea house. A year later, the dainty tearoom opened. But it simply wasn't big enough for all the activities and good deeds in which the women of the improvement society wished to participate. By 1916, a new teahouse, on nearby Monument Street, had been built, used in winter as a community house where courses in home nursing, rug making, and cooking were offered. Over time, a bookshop, stationery store, and clothing store were added to the teahouse. Today, only the teahouse remains, serving luncheon as well as afternoon tea in a sunny old-fashioned dining room with lace curtains at the windows and porcelain plates decorating the walls. From the teahouse and its garden, where tea is also served, diners can view the town square, where a statue of a Civil War soldier stands.

The tea is served in pots and poured into porcelain cups. As they have for nearly a century, scones with clotted cream and strawberry jam, and deviled ham, cucumber, and chutney cream cheese tea sandwiches, along with lemon tea bread, are on the menu. Tea-related gift items and teahouse-prepared foods are sold in the entryway.

WILSON FARMS

10 PLEASANT STREET, LEXINGTON

☎ (781) 862-3900

🚗 ROUTE 2 WEST FROM TO EXIT 56

DAILY 9AM TO 8PM (MAY-OCTOBER);

DAILY EXCEPT TUESDAY 9AM TO 7PM

(NOVEMBER-APRIL)

✦

*A*S ITS SHOPPING BAGS ATTEST, THE WIL-
SON FAMILY HAS BEEN OPERATING THEIR
farm since 1884. It lies a little less than twenty
miles northwest of Boston and just two miles from
the place where, on April 18, 1775, the Minutemen
were attacked by British Redcoats on the Lexington
Green. Here, thirty-nine acres of profitable fields
stretch, providing much of the produce for the post-
and-beam farm store that is frequented year-round
by lovers of fresh vegetables, fruit, and eggs.

James Alexander Wilson, who hailed from Inn-
iskillen, Northern Ireland, first farmed this land,
originally as a tenant farmer until he was able to
buy sixteen acres of the land he had been working. To assure that he had crisp cabbages, turnips,
and celery to market throughout the winter, he dug
underground pits to store the vegetables under lay-
ers of salt hay to insulate them. He talked his fellow

farmers into bringing him their produce, too, so he would have a full wagon of fresh vegetables to take to Boston's Quincy Market early in the morning. A full wagon, he said, always made a good impression on buyers.

The farm did well, and two of James Alexander's sons took it over. It prospered until the Depression and World War II. Then, for a time, the family market garden barely supported their two families. But in 1952, the Wilsons decided to open a roadside stand, and people flocked to it.

Today, Alan and Don Wilson, who are cousins and grandsons of founder James Alexander, and three of their sons run the family farm, selling not only fruits and vegetables but also baked goods, flowers, cheeses, delicatessen items, eggs, and turkeys in season. In 1955, the Wilsons began buying small farms 35 miles away in neighboring New Hampshire to have even more produce to sell. They now have 600 New Hampshire acres.

In addition to the produce they grow out of doors, the Wilsons have two greenhouses, and, just as their grandfather did more than 100 years ago, they buy from others what they can't grow themselves. These days that might be red peppers from Holland or oranges from Israel.

YE OLDE PEPPER COMPANIE

122 DERBY STREET, SALEM

☎ (978) 745-2744

🚆 COMMUTER RAIL FROM NORTH STATION

DAILY 10AM TO 5PM

✦

A SHIPWRECK STARTED IT ALL. IN 1806, MARY
SPENCER AND HER YOUNG SON SET SAIL
from England for America with everything they
owned, looking forward to a new life across the Atlantic. But the ship was wrecked and the Spencers, with
little more than what they were wearing, arrived in
Salem. They managed to find a place to stay on Buffum Street in North Salem, but they were penniless.
Mrs. Spencer let it be known, however, that she was
something of a candy maker, and so her new neigh-
bors supplied her with a barrel of sugar.

In no time at all—so the story goes—using a
recipe she had obtained from a sailor on her trans-
atlantic crossing, Mrs. Spencer combined the sugar
with water, cream of tartar, cornstarch, and oil of
peppermint to make a hard white candy that she
called Gibraltars. (The sailor who provided the recipe was Egyptian, according to the legend, and the
candy, in its original wrapping and turned on its
side, resembled a mummy.) Piling her Gibraltars

into a pail, Mrs. Spencer sold them each day from the steps of Salem's old First Church, which today is the Daniel Lowe Building.

Her Gibraltars were an instant success. Not only were they flavorful, but they never grew stale. (One that has been preserved in a glass case for two hundred years was tasted fifty years ago. It reportedly still melted in the mouth as a Gibraltar should.)

Gibraltars were so popular that local businesses advertised the name on placards in their shop windows to draw customers. Mrs. Spencer soon was able to give up selling on the church steps. She bought a horse and wagon and peddled her candy from door to door. On her death, her son inherited the business, but he kept it only briefly before returning to England around 1830.

The candy operation's buyer was George Pepper, who continued to make the popular Gibraltars in a factory he opened on Buffum Street, selling them from a store on North Street. Pepper developed a new candy, too—the Black Jack, a stick candy made from blackstrap molasses that is said to have been the first of its kind made in America. About 1900 he hired George Burkinshaw to work with him.

Today, Burkinshaw's great grandson, Robert, his wife, Christine, and their children, Craig and Jaclyn, are still making diamond-shaped Gibraltars and

Black Jack stick candies from the original recipes. Ye Olde Pepper Companie also sells old-fashioned honey horehound slugs, horehound squares, clove and anise drops, and peppermint and spearmint kisses.

The sweet-toothed will delight in the jars of colorful chocolate, cherry, orange, tangerine, sour apple, butterscotch, and grape candy sticks on the store's shelves, too. The shop's present site, in a former grocery store, is as historic as the candies—it's just across the street from the House of the Seven Gables, made famous by nineteenth-century Salem writer, Nathaniel Hawthorne.

In Brief

BOSCHETTO'S BAKERY, 158 SALEM STREET, BOSTON. Just across the street from the Old North Church, where the signal lanterns for Paul Revere hung in the belfry in 1775, old-time bakers bake crusty Italian bread all night at Boschetto's. They still do the baking—126 loaves at a time—in the same brick oven that Andrew Boschetto installed when he opened the bakery in 1905 after arriving from southern Italy. Until 1965, the bakery stayed in the Boschetto family. Today its baker-owner is Bartolomeo De Stefano.

MARTIGNETTI LIQUORS, 64 CROSS STREET, BOSTON. Italian groceries, breads, and imported olive oils were the stock in trade of Carmine Anthony Martignetti when he opened a shop on Salem Street in the North End in 1908. But when it looked as if Prohibition was nearing its end, he decided to expand beyond food items and applied for and received Liquor License Number One from the city of Boston. In 1933, wine and malt beverages joined the groceries on the store's shelves. In the 1950s, Martignetti's went into the wholesale as well as retail business, establishing its wholesale operation in Watertown. (Today it is located in Norwood.) Also in the 1950s, the Salem Street retail store moved to Cross Street. In 1987, Martignetti's stopped carrying groceries as it opened other retail stores in Brighton and Chelsea.

HARDWARE STORES & LOCKSMITHS

✦

CHARLES W. BENTON COMPANY

230 FRIEND STREET, BOSTON

☎ (617) 523-0787

🚋 MBTA GREEN OR ORANGE LINE TO
NORTH STATION

MONDAY-FRIDAY 8AM TO 5PM

✦

*I*N THE SHADOW OF NORTH STATION AND THE BOSTON GARDEN, CHARLES W. BENTON COMpany has made keys and serviced locks since 1898. Sometimes the company was called Benton the Locksmith, sometimes C.W. Benton Locksmith, sometimes The Old Keyhole.

When Swedish-born Charles Benton bought the company, it had already been in existence for twenty-eight years, so he proudly put over the door of his lock shop "Established in 1870." A few years earlier, at age thirty, Benton, tired of shoveling coal on tramp steamers as a way to see the world, had apprenticed himself to a New York locksmith to learn the trade before moving to Boston and buying the business. The shop was located then on Lancaster Street, just a few blocks away from its present location.

In 1949, Ezio Maestranzi, a knife grinder from Guistino, Italy, bought the shop—then at 110 Portland Street—from him. Maestranzi, in his EZ Sharpening truck, had previously been a traveling knife-sharpener. When, in 1962, as part of redevelopment, the city took over the Portland Street location, Benton's moved to Friend Street.

Today it is a cubbyhole of a place filled with gleaming brass and porcelain doorknobs, safes, mailboxes, mail slots, doorknockers, security boxes, keys, and key chains. The Maestranzi children have operated the business since 1976.

BOSTON LOCK & SAFE CO.

30 LINCOLN STREET, BRIGHTON

☎ (617) 787-3400

🚌 MBTA BUS #86 TO MARKET STREET
AND BIRMINGHAM PARKWAY

MONDAY-FRIDAY 8:30AM TO 5PM

✦

*M*AGICIANS, ESCAPE ARTISTS, INVENTORS—AND POLICE—HAVE, DOWN THROUGH THE years, been customers of this lock and safe company that was started on North Street in Boston in 1789, the year that George Washington became president.

James and Thomas Winship, whitesmiths (locksmiths and tinsmiths in today's parlance), began importing locks and hardware from England to Boston in Revolutionary days. Eventually they expanded the company to include leather goods, trunks, clock parts, carriage hardware, and, eventually, safes.

In about 1900, Vargel Stoia, a priest of the Albanian Rite, emigrated to America. To supplement his clergyman's income, Stoia, who in time had fourteen children to support, went to work for the Winships' company. Cutting keys became his specialty, and he succeeded in making Winship's one of the largest suppliers of cut keys and blanks for luggage in the world. In time, he became the company's owner.

His son, James, who succeeded him, reportedly numbered among his friends the escape artist Harry Houdini. Whenever the magician performed in Boston, James made a point of being there. His son, Harry, was so entranced with his father's Houdini tales that, when he was just fourteen, he decided he would become an escape artist, too.

For the next five years he practiced the trade, escaping from locked trunks and unshackling himself from handcuffs at social functions and fraternal club meetings. But one day, shackled to a radiator, the key that should have freed him failed to work, and his hands became severely burned. Harry decided it was time to go to college and then into the family business.

With the same flamboyance he had exhibited as a magician, he had "Mr. Lock" printed on his car license plate. He also opened a small museum in one of the company showrooms to display Houdini posters as well as handcuffs and straitjackets said to have been Houdini's.

But although entranced with magic, he also saw to it that the firm flourished, eventually moving it from downtown Boston to Brighton. Today his sons, David and Theodore, sell high-security locks and install safes, bank and jewelry vaults, museum, bank, and locker locks, and electronic security systems throughout New England. They have been called upon to repair safes that thieves have tried to blow up or pry open, and to work on locks in jails. Once, when a frantic airline passenger lost the key to her cat's carrying case, they were asked to send a locksmith to the airport to unlock it (and nearly opened a look-alike case with a hissing snake inside).

The company has been variously named the Boston Safe Co., Boston Lock, Boston Lock & Clock, and Boston Lock & Key before taking its present name of Boston Lock & Safe.

E. R. BUTLER & CO.

38 CHARLES STREET, BOSTON
☎ (617) 722-0230
🚊 MBTA RED LINE TO CHARLES-MGH; OR
MBTA RED OR GREEN LINE TO PARK STREET
TUESDAY-SATURDAY 10AM TO 6PM

✦

*A*T THE TURN OF THE TWENTIETH CENTURY WHEN WASHINGTON STREET, NEAR THE HARbor and ship chandleries, was the hardware center of Boston, Walter C. Vaughan, with several others, established a general hardware business in 1902, the J.D. Jewett Company. But Vaughan had bigger ideas than dealing with mere run-of-the-mill hardware. It seemed to him that owners of the fine old residences of Boston might like ornamental brass doorknobs, hinge plates, and locks that would enhance the special quality of their homes.

Vaughan began collecting antique hardware from the Colonial and Federal periods and traveled extensively, searching for European hardware. In 1909, he broke away from the general hardware company and founded his own high-end firm, W.C. Vaughan. A year later, he began manufacturing reproductions.

Enoch Robinson of Somerville, nearly a century earlier, had been the first designer of decorative hardware in America, supplying locks, knobs, and bolts for the Old City Hall, the State House, and the Parker House. (In Washington, D.C., there are still Robinson fixtures on doors at the United States Treasury.) Until Robinson began making builder's decorative hardware, including doorknobs, hinges, locks, doorstops, latches, and fasteners, all such hardware had been imported from Europe. An apocryphal story has it that Robinson, seeking to make his crystal doorknobs the only ones customers could buy, would snatch up shipments of such doorknobs arriving from abroad and bury them in his backyard. Hardware like Robinson's was just what Vaughan needed for his store, so he acquired Robinson's company, then owned by L.S. Hall, who had been Vaughan's shop foreman. Hall came along, too.

Over the years, W.C. Vaughan Company moved innumerable times and acquired many talented draftsmen. One of these was Elmer Pratt, who joined the company in the 1930s, and to whom Vaughan ultimately gave his firm. In 2000, W.C. Vaughan became the property of E.R. Butler & Company of New York, but the fine hardware it sells continues to be manufactured near Boston, in Braintree.

In the days when Vaughan established his company, he was noted for the way he mounted samples invitingly and put his wares in homelike settings. Today, his successor, E.R. Butler, pays the same attention to display, and the company's brass-plated doorknobs and locks, whether nickel, brass, copper, silver, or gold, are all artistically mounted.

And W.C. Vaughan was quite right—the owners of Victorian Back Bay townhouses have been willing to pay premium prices for just the right hardware. Today a single doorknob can cost between $150 and $450 if it is the perfect match for their historic homes. There are even some customers (though they are few) who will spend as much as $900 for a hand-engraved, hand-hammered, gold-plated knob.

DICKSON BROS. CO.

26 BRATTLE STREET, CAMBRIDGE
☎ (617) 876-6760
🚊 MBTA RED LINE TO HARVARD SQUARE
MONDAY-FRIDAY 8:30AM TO 6PM; SATURDAY
8:30AM TO 5:30PM; SUNDAY 10AM TO 4PM

✦

*E*D VER PLANCK, THE CURRENT OWNER OF DICKSON'S HARDWARE, IS NOT CERTAIN OF the history of the hardware store he has owned since 1963, but he does know that a series of owners have traced the store back to at least 1906.

Situated in the heart of Harvard Square, Dickson's has been the favorite hardware store of such Cambridge notables as Watergate prosecutor Archibald Cox, economist John Kenneth Galbraith, and celebrity chef Julia Child. With a big canvas bag slung over her arm, Child often could be seen walking the narrow aisles of Dickson's, selecting just what she needed, and popping it into her bag—often to the dismay of customers who thought she was shoplifting. She wasn't, of course. Filling up her canvas bag and then dumping everything out at the cash register was the way she liked to shop. Her famous kitchen is now on display at the Smithsonian Institution in Washington, D.C.; prominently displayed

[100]

in it is a red drain board from Dickson's.

The three-story emporium carries everything an old-fashioned hardware store should—flowerpots and teakettles and Pyrex ware, window shades and paints and hardware of all sorts. Employees sharpen knives and cut keys and provide another service hard to come by nowadays—making sturdy radiator covers to order.

MASSE HARDWARE

249 WALDEN STREET, CAMBRIDGE
☎ (617) 876-3463
🚇 MBTA RED LINE TO PORTER SQUARE
MONDAY, TUESDAY, THURSDAY, FRIDAY 8AM
TO 6PM; WEDNESDAY 8AM TO 1PM;
SATURDAY 8AM TO 5PM

✦

BACK IN 1881, NINETEEN-YEAR-OLD FRANCIS XAVIER MASSE, WITH JUST TWENTY BOR-rowed dollars in his pocket, left his hometown in Quebec to seek his fortune in the United States. An enterprising youth, he had, earlier, at the age of twelve, decided there was no future for him on the family farm and had gone to Quebec City, where he found work in a grocery store. There he had earned enough both to send money home and to pay to be tutored in English. In those days, many a French Canadian, eager to escape the farm life that seemed inevitable at home, came to work in the clay pits of Cambridge's New England Brick Company. The train from Quebec City made a stop for them at the Brickyard Crossing Station.

Young Masse got off the train at that stop and walked up Sherman Street in the direction of Harvard Square. Tempting fragrances assailed him from a bakery. Hungry after his long trip, he went in. Before he left, he had a job in Peter Morse's bakery.

But the bakery was not prospering, and two years after Masse was hired in 1883, he was told that it would soon be closing. Masse asked his boss if he would let him run it for a year, feeling sure he could turn the business around, and, having a good business sense, that is exactly what he did. By 1886, when the bakery and several neighboring properties were burned in a fire, Peter Morse had it rebuilt because, by then, it was doing so well. By 1888, Masse had also married his boss's daughter, Lydia.

Soon after, realizing he would have a family to support, Masse decided he would do better with a general store than a bakery. He was right, and the general store thrived until World War I. Then he converted it into a hardware store.

Meanwhile, Masse had become a pillar of the community. He was a founder and first president of the North Cambridge Cooperative Bank and helped establish two churches in the neighborhood. When French Marshal Ferdinand Foch, who had been in charge of British, French, and American forces in the war, came to Harvard to speak, Francis Xavier Masse was asked to be his interpreter.

As he grew older, Frederick, one of his 16 children, took over the business, though Francis Xavier continued to work in the store until he was 91. Frederick's son, David, although he studied physics, decided halfway through Boston College that his heart was really in the hardware store. He is its current owner-proprietor.

Every inch of Masse Hardware's wall space is taken up with hardware—scrapers and chisels, locks and pulleys, doorknobs of porcelain, brass, and wood, shovel handles, light fixtures, and plumbing fixtures. The motto of the store is "If we don't have it, you don't need it." Masse's carries hardware for the old homes of Cambridge, too. There are bolts to put antique beds together and weights and sash chains for the windows of yesterday. The store's nail bin holds fifty-four 100-pound kegs of nails (but if a customer wants only one, he can buy just that). Though it has rarely happened, if a customer has discovered something Masse's doesn't have, and really needs it, David Masse has made it for him.

VANDERHOOF HARDWARE COMPANY

28 MAIN STREET, CONCORD

☎ (978) 369-2243

🚆 COMMUTER RAIL FROM NORTH STATION

MONDAY-FRIDAY 8AM TO 5:30PM;

SATURDAY UNTIL 5PM

✦

*I*N 1904, WHEN ALBERT VANDERHOOF FIRST SAW IT, THIS MAIN STREET STORE WAS M.L. Hatch's stove dealership. Vanderhoof, an enterprising bookkeeper for a Somerville hardware store, made an offer to buy the Concord store. He next purchased the Somerville store's stock and moved that to Concord.

With the range of Glenwood products Hatch had carried—cast-iron ranges, parlor stoves, and pull-chain toilets—along with an extensive stock of hardware from the Somerville store, Vanderhoof had a new enterprise. His gold and black sign over the door read: "Albert Vanderhoof. Hardware, Plumbing & Heating."

Down through the years, there have been few changes in the layout at Vanderhoof's. Now as then, the 138 handmade drawers that line the north wall are filled with hooks and eyes, hinges, sash locks, coat hooks, eyebolts, and screw eyes. There still is a rolling ladder to get to the top shelves. Every kind of carpenter's equipment, whether hammers and nails and wrenches or wood glue, paint, and stain, can be found at Vanderhoof's. Two aisles are lined with kitchen necessities such as custard cups, muffin tins, and pancake turners, along with contemporary electrical appliances.

Just in case a northeaster boils up the Atlantic seaboard and visits Concord, kerosene and gas lamps are for sale as they used to be, as well as Sterno for boiling water if the power or gas goes out.

Albert Vanderhoof's great-grandson, Scott, is now the owner of the store and his nephew, Tom, a fifth-generation Vanderhoof who is a college student, takes over in Scott's absence. Although real estate is at a premium in Concord, the Vanderhoof family has been able to hold onto the business because Albert, more than a century ago, was canny enough to buy the portion of the building which houses the business.

In Brief

SWARTZ TRUE VALUE HARDWARE, 353 WATERTOWN STREET, NEWTON. Originally a general store founded in 1890 by a German immigrant and his wife, Swartz Hardware moved into this building in 1900. Jacob and Julia Swartz sold wooden kegs and casks, toys, and household goods. They filled customers' empty milk bottles with kerosene for their stoves and made deliveries door-to-door from a horse-drawn wagon. But Swartz soon turned to providing the mills of this mill town with essential items such as wooden forks (used to stir cloth during processing to avoid static electricity), as well as valves and plumbing parts for mill machinery. Today, under the ownership of its founder's grandson, Michael Swartz, Swartz is a full-scale hardware, household goods, and garden store, four times the size it was when it was a general store with a pot-bellied stove.

JEWELERS

✦

LONG'S

100 SUMMER STREET, BOSTON
☎ (617) 426-8500
🚆 MBTA SILVER, ORANGE, OR RED LINE TO
DOWNTOWN CROSSING
MONDAY-FRIDAY 9:30AM TO 6PM;
SATURDAY 10AM TO 5PM

✦

SOON AFTER THE END OF THE WAR OF 1812, BOSTON BEGAN ITS RISE AS A LEADING AMERican shipping and mercantile center. By the 1840s, it was prosperous, indeed, in shipbuilding as well as foreign trade. It was in Boston that the speedy clipper ships that carried cargo to and from the Far East were designed and constructed. Such English literary notables as Charles Dickens came to visit the city and were received with much fanfare. The Cunard Steamship Line, in 1840, began carrying passengers between Boston and England and in the 1850s, English novelist William Makepeace Thackeray was one of those on board.

By the 1870s the city began to be known as the Athens of America. The *Atlantic Monthly* began publication in Boston; The Old Corner Bookstore on School and Washington Streets became a gathering place for such writers as William Wadsworth

Longfellow, Ralph Waldo Emerson, Nathaniel Hawthorne, and Oliver Wendell Holmes; and the Boston Public Library and the Music Hall were attracting many. In those post Civil War Days, it was the liveliest of places culturally and economically. By then its streets were paved and, in the late 1870s, a sewer system was developed so flooded walkways and animal waste no longer had to be navigated. Downtown buildings were filled with cargoes of wool and cotton and furniture ready to be shipped to distant ports.

Then, at 7:24 on the night of Saturday, November 9, 1872, an alarm rang out from a firebox at the corner of Summer and Kingston Streets. Firemen rushed to the scene, but the water supply was insufficient to quench the fire. The city's fire horses were suffering from an epidemic, and many of the engines had to be hand-pulled. Downtown buildings, where dry goods were often stored in wooden lofts, were soon ablaze. Gas mains exploded. Not until the early hours of Monday was the conflagration finally put out. By then, 776 buildings between Washington Street and the waterfront were destroyed. The damage was estimated at $60 million.

But jeweler Thomas Long Jr. was lucky. The firm he had opened two years earlier in downtown Boston escaped the ravages of the fire by half a block. His business was largely a wholesale costume jewelry operation that took advantage of Boston's proximity to Providence and Attleboro, which were the centers of costume jewelry manufacturing at the time. Salesmen from the Long Company traveled by rail throughout the New England states carrying their wares from city to city, setting up showrooms in hotels where well-heeled customers could see their latest jewelry lines.

Among Long's salesmen in the mid-1870s were two New Hampshire natives, then living in Newtonville, Frank and Charles Davidson, who became the company's owners after Long's death in 1890. Six years later the brothers expanded the business by opening a retail store at 77 Summer Street. Soon, in addition to costume jewelry, Long's was selling diamonds and gold, watches, silver, and gifts, and in 1922, the jewelry store settled in at 40-46 Summer Street. It remained there for seventy-five years until 2004 in a building with a cast-iron front that was one of the first to rise after the 1872 fire.

Long's retained its wholesale and department store businesses as well, however. During the Depression it was this wholesale business that kept the firm going. Business quickly rebounded when the economy improved, and by 1936, Long's was back to dealing in diamonds. As Bostonians began to move to the suburbs in the 1950s, Long's, always a company that kept up with the times and by then in the hands of a third generation—Frank Jr. and Allen—began opening branch stores.

Until 1980, Long's stayed in Davidson hands. Then it was sold to Henry Birks & Sons of Montreal, Canada. Today it us owned by RJC Corporation of Danvers, Massachusetts, and has shops throughout Massachusetts as well as New Hampshire. As in the days of Thomas Long, however, there remains a Long's in the heart of downtown—though it is now in a modern rather than an historic building.

SHREVE, CRUMP & LOW

440 BOYLSTON STREET, BOSTON
☎ (617) 267-9100
🚊 MBTA GREEN LINE TO ARLINGTON OR COPLEY
MONDAY-SATURDAY 10AM TO 6PM; THURSDAY
10AM TO 7PM; SUNDAY NOON TO 5PM

✦

*I*N 1796, WHEN SALEM SILVERSMITH JOHN MCFARLANE OPENED A SHOP SELLING "SILVER-ware, watches, and jewelry" on Marlborough Street (today's Washington Street at Downtown Crossing) it was hardly a gamble. Boston was the largest port in the nation, with more shipping trade than in Philadelphia and New York combined, and there were money and customers in abundance.

The business was soon thriving, known for its fine jewelry and the grandest of presentation objects. In 1835 the citizens of Boston commissioned a thirty-pound sterling silver vase from the company to honor orator Daniel Webster. In 1840, the firm designed and executed a sterling cup embellished with cockleshells and dolphin handles to welcome Britain's Cunard Line when it opened a Boston office. And in 1899, the company created the Davis Cup for tennis at the request of Harvard graduate and tennis aficionado Dwight F. Davis. In addition,

[114]

the firm sold the finest of antiques to Boston house-holds and supplied the china, crystal, and silver for virtually all of the city's brides-to-be. When, in the 1850s, gas lighting was invented, the company created decorative gaslights for such establishments as the Parker House hotel and Trinity Church.

The partners who gave the firm its names were John J. Low, of a Salem shipping family; Benjamin Shreve Jr., also of Salem, whose expert eye found many of the antiques the company sold; and much-traveled buyer and salesman Charles H. Crump. He once managed to bring back—for a Back Bay home—a balcony from the Tuileries Palace in Paris; he convinced King Kalakau of Hawaii to buy the gaslights for his palace from Shreve Crump & Low, along with $20,000 worth of silverware and bric-a-brac.

By 1872, the elegant store, at the corner of Washington and Summer Streets, was acclaimed as "without equal in the world." Its showcases were in Elizabethan style, its counters painted white and gold, its ceilings frescoed.

But on November 9 of that year, Boston's Great Fire started in a warehouse in the heart of downtown. Instead of burning to the ground, Shreve, Crump & Low, with all its gas lamps, exploded. (Boston legend has it that Phillips Brooks, author of the Christmas carol "O Little Town of Bethlehem," and rector of neighboring Trinity Church—which was also destroyed—saved some of the jewelry store's riches for the company by stuffing them into his coat pockets and top hat to get them out of the exploding building.)

But Shreve, Crump & Low quickly recovered, constructing "a jeweled palace of the trade," once again on Washington Street. The design of this store made use of artificial lighting and plate glass in innovative ways. Two enormous windows lined with crimson velvet became showcases for statuary, bronzes, jewelry, and paintings. Newspaper accounts of the day described the main showroom as "palatial" where the "richness of the fittings is at once perceptible, although it is not obtrusively so." To show off the most expensive silverware, a retail department that resembled an art gallery was created and hung with sixteenth and seventeenth-century tapestries and filled with marble and bronze statues and furniture "of harmonious design." At the end of a hall was a brilliantly lit room where the silverware was in showcases whose glass reflected the dazzling artificial light.

In 1891, Shreve, Crump & Low moved yet again, this time to larger premises at the corner of Tremont and West Streets. The new building was described as "the most elegant store in the Hub." Boston art collector Isabella Stewart Gardner became a customer, buying, on one shopping expedition, a set of four diamond and amethyst brooches and stickpins.

In 1929, the store had an Art Deco structure designed for it at the corner of Boylston and Arlington Streets. This incarnation, acclaimed for its "tasteful modernism," was in great contrast with the ornate décor of its previous home. At this site, the owners had safes built underneath Boylston Street to hold some of the store's most valuable items.

During the ownership of Canadians Ann and Kim Birks, Shreve, Crump & Low moved again in 2005. It now occupies a modern building at the corner of Boylston and Berkeley, and a hand-blown two-story high Steuben glass sculpture called "Last Night the Rain Spoke to Me," is the store's centerpiece. Still, reflections of its historic past can be seen in the French Lalique light fixtures, Lalique table, mid-eighteenth-century grandfather's clock, and the watercolors of jewelry, made on wax paper by the designers of another era, that decorate its walls.

Today its owner is Chestnut Hill gem dealer David Walker, owner of David & Co.. Since 1974, in addition to its downtown location, Shreve, Crump & Low has had a Chestnut Hill store at 169 Boylston Street in the Mall.

In Brief

E. B. HORN, 429 WASHINGTON STREET AT DOWN-
TOWN CROSSING, BOSTON. Located in one of Boston's few surviving mid-nineteenth-century Greek
Revival granite commercial buildings, the E.B. Horn
jewelry company has conducted business on this site
since 1878. In 1839, Edwin B. Horn, a watch, clock,
and lamp maker as well as jeweler, opened for business on Hanover Street. His wife brought the silver-
smithing tradition to the marriage—she was the
daughter of renowned Newburyport silver manufacturer A.J. Towle. Now, as then, E.B. Horn (currently
owned by Michael, Richard, and Philip Finn) sells
and repairs watches and fine jewelry. It also deals in
estate and designer jewelry and sterling and plated
silver hollowware.

SIMPSON'S INC., 44 TEMPLE PLACE, BOSTON.
Simpson's Inc. has been an estate buyer since 1898.
Sam Bellar, who first opened this store in 1898 in the
Jewelers' Building on Washington Street, called it
Simpson's after a notable old English money-lending
family. (Bellar himself was a Pole from the Polish-
Russian border.) Today his grandson, Ross Bellar,
buys and sells estate jewelry and is a pawnbroker.

MUSICAL INSTRUMENT MAKERS

✦

WM. S. HAYNES CO., INC.

12 PIEDMONT STREET, BOSTON
☎ (617) 482-7456
🚇 MBTA GREEN LINE TO ARLINGTON
MONDAY-FRIDAY 9AM TO 4PM BY APPOINTMENT

✦

*F*OR A SERIOUS NINETEENTH-CENTURY AMER-
ICAN FLUTIST, IT WASN'T EASY TO OBTAIN a
quality instrument. They were made almost exclu-
sively in Paris and Munich, and could take as long
as a year to have in hand, from placing an order to
having the instrument made and sent by ship. In the
1890s, William Sherman Haynes, an amateur flutist as well as a silversmith, and his brother, George,
were talked by flutist-friends into trying their hand
at flute making. Since all good flutes had silver keys,
and since the very best of flutes—for the quality of
the sound—were of precious metals, it made sense
that silversmiths should be able to make them.

It wasn't, of course, quite that easy. First the
brothers had to learn how to make musical instruments. They went to work for a time for J. C. Haynes
(no relation), a leading instrument importer and
manufacturer. By 1900, William and George had
learned enough to be making flutes of their own and
to have a shop on Washington Street.

Until 1976, the firm stayed in the Haynes family. Today, Eastman Strings of Baltimore, Maryland, is the owner, but changes in ownership have not changed the way Haynes flutes are made.

They are still entirely hand-crafted, each one requiring eighty to one hundred hours of work, and the forging machine from the company's earliest days continues to play a role in flute production. The site of the workshop today is a 160-year-old former carriage house in a neighborhood of early nineteenth-century red-brick townhouses.

Between 250 and 300 flutes are made annually at Haynes's, and only in gold, silver, and platinum. They range in price from $7,000 for a silver flute to $40,000 for one made in platinum. (The company also makes a few wooden piccolos.)

All parts of each flute except the tubing are made and assembled on the premises. To assure that the sound is perfect, a professional flutist plays each instrument before it is released. Most flutes are made to order, and the orders come from all over the world. The company also does repairs.

In the reception room of the cozy little shop, memorabilia of the Hayneses is on display. There are table-sized figures of Pan and His Pipes from Mrs. William Haynes's antiques collection. (These were designed by Frederic MacMonnies, whose controversial statue of a naked Bacchante with Infant Faun was deemed too risqué for public display at the neighboring Boston Public Library for nearly a century.) William Haynes's gold watch sits in a case among miniature figures of flutists, while on the walls hang photographs of famous players of Haynes flutes.

In its quiet peacefulness, the Bay Village neighborhood of narrow tree-shaded streets that is home to Haynes Flutes seems most appropriate for the time-honored craft of fine flute making.

M. STEINERT & SONS

162 BOYLSTON STREET, BOSTON

☎ (617) 426-1900

🚇 MBTA GREEN LINE TO BOYLSTON OR ARLINGTON

MONDAY-THURSDAY 9AM TO 6PM;

FRIDAY, SATURDAY 9AM TO 5PM

✦

*M*ORRIS STEINERT & SONS WAS A MUSI-CAL PRESENCE IN BOSTON AND BEYOND by 1896. So the German immigrant felt comfortable taking the unusual step of building his new piano emporium, Steinert Hall, on Boylston Street, rather than Washington, which was nicknamed Piano Row for its many music stores. Steinert put his eighteen-year-old son Alexander in charge of the new store, to be assisted by his younger brother, Frederick. The six-story building, with its imposing stone façade, was an instant success, drawing pianists from all over Boston. In 1897, with horse-drawn carriages rumbling along Boylston Street's cobblestones, Alexander Steinert built a recital hall in the building's basement where performers could sing and play unaffected by street noises.

Morris Steinert had come a long way. He arrived in America from Bavaria in 1850 and made his start as a door-to-door salesman of optical goods. But he much preferred music. He played the piano, organ, and violin and soon had jobs teaching music, repairing instruments, and selling in a retail music store in Savannah, Georgia. When the Civil War began he came North, settling first in New Haven, Connecticut. He taught music, worked as a church organist, and eventually founded the Steinert Family Orchestra, which became the New Haven Symphony. He also began building pianos in 1865, but his factory failed. Then he persuaded fellow-German immigrant Heinrich Steinway, a successful piano manufacturer, to sell him a dealership. He eventually became a successful piano retailer, going on to open a piano store in Providence, Rhode Island, in 1878, and others throughout New England in addition to Steinert Hall.

In 1897, sixteen-year-old Jerome F. Murphy went to work for the Steinert firm as bookkeeper. In time he became the company's general manager and, in 1936, its owner. Today his grandsons, Paul E. Murphy Jr. and Jerome F. Murphy III own Steinert's, which, except for Denton, Cottier, & Daniels in Buffalo, New York, is the oldest Steinway piano dealership in the world. It preceded Steinert by fourteen months, thanks to the ease of transporting pianos via the Erie Canal.

Three of the six stories of the Steinert Building are devoted to selling new and used pianos, to repairing and tuning them, and for studios for piano teachers. Piano recitals are also held. When Boston's Symphony Hall is being readied for a concert and the pianists on the program need a Steinway because they have not brought their own or one is not yet available to them in Symphony Hall, they will often go to Steinert's to practice. Pianists Sergei Rachmaninoff, Ignace Paderewski, Arthur Rubinstein, and Rudolf Serkin are among those who have played or practiced in this hall over the years.

In the high-ceilinged street-floor showroom, busts of Beethoven, Brahms, Mozart, Steinway, and Chickering look down on Steinway grand and upright pianos along with Boston, Essex, Kohler, and Campbell pianos—and even digital electric pianos that are sold today.

SPORTING GOODS STORES

✦

NEW BALANCE

40 LIFE STREET, BRIGHTON

☎ (877) 623-7867 OR (617) 783-4000

🚊 MBTA RED LINE TO HARVARD THEN BUS #501

MONDAY-SATURDAY 9:30AM TO 7PM;

SUNDAY NOON TO 6PM

✦

*I*N HIS OFFICE IN DOWNTOWN BOSTON'S PEL-
HAM HOTEL IN 1906, SHOEMAKER-INVENTOR
William J. Riley, an English immigrant, always kept
a chicken's foot on his desk. It was there to demon-
strate to his customers how his New Balance Arch,
designed with three points of support in the shape
of a triangle, had been inspired by watching the per-
fectly balanced three-clawed feet of the chickens he
kept in his Belmont yard.

In 1927, Riley was doing well enough with his
arch supports to hire a commissioned salesman,
Arthur Hall, to sell them. Hall traveled throughout Massachusetts and Rhode Island with Riley's
supports, always making sure that he stopped at
police departments, fire stations, and post offices
where the employees were on their feet all day. By
1929 business was so good that Riley patented his
arch supports; four years later, he made Hall a part
owner in his concern.

The company somehow managed to survive the Depression, and by the end of the 1930s, with demand for his arch supports increasing, Riley moved his business to larger quarters in Cambridge. There he began thinking about making athletic footwear, and one day in 1938, when a local running club was having a workout at the Belmont High School track, Riley stopped by to tell the young runners how he could make running shoes for them that would be more comfortable and more serviceable. He measured their feet and promised that if the shoes he made were not satisfactory, the boys would not have to pay for them. Two weeks later, he returned with the promised running shoes made of light but sturdy kangaroo leather—and with the arch supports inside.

Word of the new shoes spread, and by 1941, New Balance was also making, in addition to the running shoes, baseball, basketball, tennis, and boxing shoes with Riley's signature arch supports. In time, the company moved to Watertown.

In 1949, Riley retired and in 1953, Hall sold the company for $10,000 to his daughter and son-in-law, Eleanor and Paul Kidd. In the basement of their Arlington home, Paul Kidd soon went to work to improve New Balance's running shoe.

Today owned by Brookline native and entrepreneur Jim Davis, the shoes inspired by a chicken's foot are sold worldwide. Since 1976, Brighton has been the company headquarters with a shop crammed with shoes and sporting goods.

ROACH'S SPORTING GOODS, INC.

1957 MASSACHUSETTS AVENUE, CAMBRIDGE

☎ (617) 876-5816

🚊 MBTA RED LINE TO PORTER SQUARE

MONDAY–SATURDAY 9AM TO 6PM;

THURSDAY TO 9PM

✦

*I*N THE EARLY YEARS OF THE NINETEENTH CENTURY, CATTLE GRAZED ON THE COMMON in North Cambridge. As the century progressed, livestock was replaced by stockyards and a slaughterhouse as well as taverns like Porter's, which, in time, gave its name both to the square and to the Porterhouse steak. French Canadians and Irish moved to this developing part of the city and stayed. Gradually, Porter Square, at the turn of the twentieth century, began to attract stores. One was Roach Hardware Company, which was opened by Charles Roach on Upland Road, just off the square. His business soon was booming. He carried not just hardware but firearms and fishing tackle, too.

When the Depression came and business plummeted, Roach was forced to let all his employees go—except for his cook, Teresa Rutledge. She gave up cooking to help him keep the store open, and when he died in 1934, he left his hardware store to her. By then she had married Joseph Callanan, who quit the railroad to join her in managing the store. The Callanans had two sons who, along with their father, were out hunting and fishing when they weren't minding the store.

And so in 1956, when the sons joined the business, they decided to play down hardware and play up sporting goods. Roach's moved a block south of the square to the sprawling, former furniture store with creaking wooden floors and high tin ceilings that has been its home ever since. The high ceilings were just right for displaying long fishing rods and hunting rifles. The company's name was changed to Roach's Sporting Goods and the hardware products were relegated to the basement.

Hanging from the ceiling are minnow nets, trout nets, and black bridge nets for bringing fish onto a boat. A stuffed wolverine and the heads of caribou, grizzly, mountain goats, and an Alaskan moose, as well as rugs made from mountain lion and wolf skins are displayed. There are hammocks, tents, gun racks, snowshoes, binoculars, Swiss Army hunting knives, plaid hunting shirts, clay pigeons, gun safes, ski masks, antique and collectible shotguns, and target rifles. Camping equipment, life jackets, boots, bug repellants, and kayaks have replaced the hardware in the basement.

Joe Callanan's grandsons, Joe and Chuck Callanan, are the store's owners now. The old Boston & Maine Railroad lantern that belonged to their grandfather is displayed prominently, near where purchases are tallied on an old-fashioned crank cash register—a reminder of how different their lives might have been if Teresa Rutledge hadn't agreed to give up cooking and gone to work in Charles Roach's hardware store a little more than a century ago.

In Brief

BRINE'S SPORTING GOODS, 4 CHURCH STREET, BELMONT. Since the late 1880s, two branches of the Brine family have operated sporting goods businesses in Cambridge and Boston. Haberdasher James W. Brine's firm began more than a century ago selling neckties. In 2004, the firm, Brine's Sporting Goods, moved to Belmont. All manner of sporting apparel are sold today.

BRINE, INC., 27 OTIS STREET, BOSTON. Meanwhile, in 1922, a nephew of James W.'s left his uncle's firm and opened his own company at this location selling athletic equipment to schools and colleges. Today it manufactures lacrosse and soccer equipment that is sold worldwide.

STONECUTTERS

✦

W.C. CANNIFF & SONS, INC.

CANNIFF MONUMENTS

531 CUMMINS HIGHWAY, ROSLINDALE

☎ (617) 323-3690

🚆 MBTA RED LINE TO MATTAPAN THEN BUS #30

ALONG CUMMINS HIGHWAY

DAILY 9AM TO 8PM

✦

DARK-GRAY QUINCY GRANITE (NO LONGER QUARRIED) HAS LONG BEEN RENOWNED. President John Adams gave land containing granite to Quincy, the town of his birth, for the construction of the First Parish Church, where he would come to be buried. Even earlier, in 1754, surface granite from Quincy was used to build Boston's King's Chapel.

But Quincy granite really came into its own in 1825, when Solomon Willard, architect of the Bunker Hill Monument, chose it after traveling three hundred miles in search of the perfect stone for the monument he had been asked to design. Once he made his selection, he purchased the quarry for $250. To remove the needed stone, engineer Gridley Bryant constructed the first commercial railway in the country in 1826. Three railways cars weighing five tons were filled with sixteen tons of granite, time after time, and hauled by horse three miles to the Neponset River. There the stone was unloaded onto barges and taken to Charlestown.

In 1896, taking advantage of Quincy's high-quality stone, William Crowley Canniff, a native of County Cork, Ireland, began using the granite, along with that from nearby Westerly, Rhode Island, to make monuments on Penn Street in Quincy. Although it produces principally cemetery monuments, W.C. Canniff & Sons, now owned by seven grandchildren of William, has made memorials for everything from one of the racehorse Sea Biscuit to war memorials and the Suffolk Downs memorial. Canniff's stonecutting continues to be done in Quincy, but since 1908, display monuments have been sold from this location in Roslindale, and since the 1950s, also at 583 Mount Auburn Street in Cambridge. Its Cambridge showroom, built in 1870, was constructed as a comfort station and waiting room for Mount Auburn Cemetery visitors who were taking the trolley. For a time it also housed the office of the superintendent of the historic cemetery.

In Brief

THOMAS CARRIGG & SONS INC., 772 LAGRANGE STREET, WEST ROXBURY. Before Thomas Carrigg from County Clare, Ireland, became a monument maker in the 1890s and opened this shop, he had been cutting stone for bridges and for the window-sills at Harvard College. Today his great-grandsons, Joseph, Thomas, and William, still operate it.

DAVIS MONUMENTS, 3859 WASHINGTON STREET, ROSLINDALE. Stone carver David Magner came from County Cork, Ireland, to Boston, in the 1860s, working for a time for a silver company before opening his own stonecutting business, Magner Monuments, in Forest Hills. In time, Nova Scotian Frederick P. Davis, a stonecutter in the Quincy quarries, got a job with him, married his daughter Mary, and, in 1895, started his own business, F.P. Davis Monuments in Mattapan. In 1907, F.P. Davis Monuments moved to the Forest Hills section of Jamaica Plain (today, Roslindale), where it has been ever since. Today it is owned by David Magner's great-grandson Paul Davis, with a partner, John Tigges. It numbers among the monuments it has made and that stand in the mid-nineteenth-century garden cemetery of Forest Hills, those of playwright Eugene O'Neill and poet E.E. Cummings.

DEVENEY & WHITE MONUMENT COMPANY, 664 GALLIVAN BOULEVARD, DORCHESTER. In 1898, Quincy was at its height as a stone-cutting center, and the Deveney family established a wholesale granite firm there, doing business principally in New York State and the Midwest. But as the quarries were closing in the 1940s, Edward P. Deveney Sr. and his son, Edward Jr., went into the retail trade, establishing businesses in Hyde Park and on Dorchester Avenue in Dorchester and, in the 1960s, here on Gallivan Boulevard in Dorchester. In the 1970s, Gerard Deveney, grandson of the founder, and his brother-in-law, Walter White, purchased the firm, then known as E.P. Deveney Granite. Today, Gerard's son, Matt, the fourth generation in the business, operates the company. Many of its monuments stand in Dorchester's wooded mid-nineteenth-century cemetery, Cedar Grove, renowned as the only cemetery in the nation through which a trolley—the Red Line's Ashmont-Mattapan trolley—runs.

TOBACCONISTS

✦

LEAVITT & PEIRCE

1316 MASSACHUSETTS AVENUE, CAMBRIDGE
☎ (617) 547-0576
🚇 MBTA RED LINE TO HARVARD SQUARE
MONDAY-SATURDAY 9AM TO 5:30PM;
THURSDAY TO 8PM

✦

*F*OR MORE THAN A CENTURY, HARVARD MEN HAVE GATHERED AT LEAVITT & PEIRCE TO enjoy a smoke of the pipe tobacco specially mixed to their tastes or to make a selection from Leavitt & Peirce's large inventory of fine cigars. They have played chess on the balcony, or, in times past, enjoyed billiards in the cellar billiard parlor.

The founder, Fred Leavitt, a big sports fan and a booster of Harvard teams, knew how to attract students. For years, when Fred S. Knapp, who had headed university athletics, and Fred W. Moore, treasurer of the Harvard Athletic Association, were its owners, Harvard students came to this shop in the heart of Harvard Square to read the football and baseball scores pasted on its windows. Here, crew members would find their rowing schedules. Until 1893, it was to Leavitt & Peirce that Harvard men came to buy their tickets to football games. And in 1886, the torchlight parade that heralded Harvard

College's 250th anniversary began at Leavitt & Peirce's door.

In 1883, Fred H. Leavitt, a tobacco merchant, and Wallace W. Peirce, a druggist, formed a partnership and opened the tobacco store in the turreted brick Hilton Block of stores. Soon they were offering their own special pipe blends, the University Mixture and the Cake Box Mixture, which was (and still is) famous for its touch of cigar leaf. In reminiscences written on its seventy-fifth anniversary, Leavitt & Peirce was heralded as "the meeting place, the club house, the crossroads of Harvard men and the archive of Harvard memories." At one point during his tenure as Harvard president from 1909 to 1933, Abbot Lawrence Lowell heard rumors that the tobacco store might be sold. He is said to have kept a close eye on it to make sure that Leavitt & Peirce fell into the right hands from the university's point of view.

Leavitt died in 1921, Peirce in 1922. By then the shop had been bought by Moore and Knapp. With their close Harvard connection, they were just the sort of owners Lowell had hoped for. The store's next owners, also Harvard men, operated the store for thirty years before selling to Paul L. MacDonald, whose son, Paul J., is the present owner.

Although the smoking lounge and the billiard

parlor are now gone, chess and checkers are still played on the balcony. Crew oars, team pictures, and old footballs adorn the walls below the high tin ceilings. Fewer cigarettes and pipes are sold than in the old days, but Leavitt & Peirce continues to blend pipe tobacco, and cigars are ever popular. And the ship's bowsprit of a Native American woman with a bouquet of cigars clutched in her hand still hangs above the front door.

L.J. PERETTI CO. INC.

2½ PARK SQUARE, BOSTON
☎ (617) 482-0218
🚋 MBTA RED LINE TO BOYLSTON
✦

LIBERO J. PERETTI, A NATIVE OF LUGANO, SWITZERLAND, OPENED PERETTI'S CUBAN Cigar Store in a loft in the North End in 1870. There he employed, housed, and fed some seventy Cuban cigar makers whom he brought into the country. While they rolled cigars, a lectore read Dickens and Thackery aloud to them in English so they could learn the language. But the era of Cuban cigar rollers on the premises ended with the advent of Social Security when small companies could not afford to pay benefits for their workers. Peretti's had to start buying cigars pre-rolled from Cuba. Still, into the 1940s, business was so good that Peretti operated five stores in the city, among them this one at Charles and Boylston Streets, just across from the Boston Common, which opened in 1938 and is the only one that remains.

When, in 1921, Peretti's son, Libero, took over, the store began blending tobaccos, and pipes were added to its inventory. After World War II, Libero's son, Robert, further expanded the pipe tobacco business and today the store prepares more than 10,000 private blends. Actor Mickey Rooney still orders his pipe tobacco from Peretti's, and in the old days, cigar-loving Edward G. Robinson was a regular.

In 1988, Stephen Willett became Robert Peretti's partner. Since 2004, Willett has run the shop alone.

Aficionados of tobacco will find, in display cases from an old apothecary shop, century-old plug cutters and tobacco scales, and lumps of meerschaum— the fossilized remains of microscopic creatures from which the bowls of meerschaum pipes are made. Cigar box covers and ribbons decorate the walls.

Outside this little tobacco shop, instead of the typical cigar-store Indian, stands a figure of Punch (the name of a brand of Cuban cigars) holding out a cigar. And for the comfort of smokers, two benches sit outside the door, while inside are three inviting leather chairs.

In Brief

MARTINI'S SMOKE SHOP, 325 HANOVER STREET, BOSTON. Italian language newspapers and magazines, comic books, cigars, cigarettes, candy, and chewing gum have been the stock in trade of this little North End shop since 1892.

ET CETERA

✦

ANIMAL RESCUE LEAGUE
OF BOSTON

10 CHANDLER STREET, BOSTON

☎ (617) 426-9170

🚇 MBTA ORANGE LINE TO BACK BAY;

GREEN LINE TO ARLINGTON STREET;

TUESDAY-THURSDAY NOON TO 8PM;

FRIDAY, SATURDAY NOON TO 5PM

✦

ONE WINTRY DAY IN 1899, SOCIALLY MINDED BOSTONIAN ANNA HARRIS SMITH PICKED UP her skirts and marched into the office of the city's most socially prestigious newspaper, the *Boston Evening Transcript.* There she hand-delivered an impassioned plea on behalf of the city's homeless and suffering animals, urging the establishment of an Animal Rescue League. "I would like to bring before your readers the great need there is of a place in some central location in the city of Boston to which cats and dogs can be taken and either provided with homes or mercifully put to death. In other cities there are such places, but in our city when we see a dog or cat in the street, we must either harden our hearts and pass it by or—if it is a cat—take a car to Brighton and carry it out to the Ellen Gifford Home for Stray Cats that is there." Immediately upon publication on January 23, 1899, responses began arriving at the paper in support of her proposal.

The following March, the Animal Rescue League of Boston was established, and a month later, its first shelter was opened on Carver Street. By the end of May, 145 animals had been cared for; by the end of its first year, the number had reached 2,595.

But Mrs. Smith wasn't satisfied with her success. Healthy animals awaiting placement with families needed a pleasanter environment than a confining city shelter, especially large animals. So she proposed a Home of Rest for Horses outside the city, finding just the country annex she sought in 1907. Called Pine Ridge, it consisted of twenty-seven rolling, wooded acres in Dedham. That year she also acquired Boston's first animal ambulance to rescue homeless and abused creatures, and established the nation's first pet cemetery. It became the burial place of polar explorer Richard Byrd's fox terrier Igloo, one of the most renowned among the more than 35,000 beloved pets laid to rest there.

In 1956, the League moved its downtown Boston headquarters from Carver to Chandler Street, where there is now a shelter, adoption headquarters, veterinary service, and a dog-training program for rescued animals.

BON TON RUG CLEANSERS INC.

81-85 COOLIDGE HILL ROAD, WATERTOWN
☎ (617) 924-6103
🚌 MBTA BUS #71 TO COOLIDGE SQUARE
MONDAY-FRIDAY 8:30AM TO 4:30PM;
SATURDAY 9 TO 11:30AM

✦

*I*N A RED-BRICK TWO-STORY STRUCTURE AT THE EDGE OF WATERTOWN NEAR HISTORIC Mount Auburn Cemetery (where poet Henry Wadsworth Longfellow, architect Charles Bulfinch, and artist Winslow Homer are buried), rug menders listen to classical music while reweaving, rehooking, and rebraiding rugs from skeins of wool in more than 1,000 shades. This thriving business was begun by Hagop Dohanian, an Armenian who arrived in Somerville as a teenager, with his widowed mother and two younger brothers, in 1901. Refugees from Turkish massacres, they entered the United States through Boston where they had relatives. After high school, Dohanian tried his hand briefly at photography before realizing that his Armenian name and heritage gave him an advantage in dealing with Oriental rugs. Although he had learned to weave from his mother, he thought he would be more successful selling rather than weaving rugs, and began going door-to-door. But the house he bought in West Somerville after his marriage to a fellow Armenian came with a barn that had cement floors and a drain. It seemed just made for washing, so he switched businesses, from selling Oriental rugs to washing them.

With his horse and buggy, Dohanian collected rugs from as far away as the North Shore. He washed them in the barn and spread them out to dry on the grass near the Boston to Somerville railroad tracks. By 1927, he was able to buy land in Watertown and build a small shop. After the hurricane of 1938 not only blew the roof off the shop but blew away the rugs inside as well, he rebuilt. Some years later a Fourth of July firecracker set his rebuilt shop on fire. Once again, he rebuilt.

Today it is not only Oriental rugs that Bon Ton mends and washes and cleans. Broadlooms and cotton and hooked and braided rugs are all cared for in the shop Hagop Dohanian's grandson and two greatgrandsons now own and operate. The only rugs for sale are those that have been unclaimed for some time. And now, as then—because it keeps the colors from running—Bon Ton lays its Oriental carpets flat on the grass outside to dry from May to October. (In winter, customers with rugs with colors that might run are asked to return in summer.)

THE LONDON HARNESS
COMPANY

60 FRANKLIN STREET, BOSTON

☎ (617)542-9234

🚋 MBTA SILVER, ORANGE, RED LINE
TO DOWNTOWN CROSSING
MONDAY-FRIDAY 9:30AM TO 6PM;
SATURDAY 10AM-4PM

✦

*T*HE YEAR AFTER PAUL REVERE GALLOPED
FROM CHARLESTOWN TO CONCORD AND LEX-
ington to warn the Minute Men that the British
were coming, Zachariah Hick (sometimes spelled
"Hicks") opened a saddle- and harness-making
shop at 38 Cornhill in Boston. He stayed there for
forty-one years and then moved to Court Street in
1817. Hicks did well and, in 1833, when he retired,
his firm was bought by an employee, Charles Mc-
Burney. From him, ownership passed to the Winship family of trunk-makers in 1842 and a year later
moved to Elm Street. Along with Hicks's saddles and
harnesses, the firm sold Winship-designed high-
domed trunks. These trunks were popular because
the curved dome prevented handlers from stacking
heavy boxes on top of them or placing them upside
down in a coach or ship's hold. The company also

sold another ingenious Winship design—ladies' suitcases that came equipped with hangers attached on the inside of the case. The luggage company remained in Winship family hands until 1973.

Meanwhile, in 1847, in Concord, New Hampshire, the harness-making shop of James R. Hill was supplying the harnesses for the horses of the Concord Coach Company that served much of northern New England. (Thirty years later, they would outfit the horses for Buffalo Bill's Wild West Show; the animals of the P.T. Barnum Circus also wore Concord harnesses.) As business increased, Hill, in 1890, decided to open a store in Boston and called it J.R. Hill & Co.

Hill branched out beyond saddles and harnesses to sell English and French leather goods such as luggage, gloves, and handbags. English-made products were becoming increasingly popular with Boston's Brahmins. To appeal to this upscale market, the firm changed its name again to Concord Harness, then to London Harness Store, and eventually to London Harness Store Company. Although its business was increasingly in personal leather goods, it continued to send representatives to those Boston homes where horses were stabled until 1930.

As automobiles changed the nature of transportation, so, too, did London Harness change. In 1912, it was advertising such products as auto trunks, tire trunks for carrying tire repair tools, and luncheon kits along with its saddles and bridles.

In 1919, the company moved to Franklin Street. It survived the Depression and a 1939 fire that destroyed much of its expensive stock. By this time, James Hill's great-grandson, Caroll Dwight, was in charge. By 1973, it was doing well enough to buy the Boston leather-goods company that had been Zachariah Hick's.

Today's high-ceilinged London Harness shop, whose contents reflect the combined legacies of Hick's, Winship's, and Hill's enterprises, is nearly untouched. It still has the old paneled walls and mahogany display cases, and Oriental scatter rugs cover its wooden floors. Glove drawers from long ago remain, as do the cushions on which ladies of decades ago rested their elbows as they tried on gloves. Until 1968, there was still a saddle maker upstairs.

In addition to the stock of fine leather goods and luggage for which London Harness has been renowned for generations, there are also such items as barometers, globes, backgammon and chess sets, dart games, picnic baskets—and, with a nod to the past—horse-head-shaped bronze bookends.

B.L. MAKEPEACE, INC.

+

*I*N 1895, TWENTY-THREE-YEAR-OLD BERTRAND L. MAKEPEACE DECIDED TO OPEN A BLUEPRINT shop on the top floor of a building at 345 Washington Street in downtown Boston.

Makepeace had started work with a blueprint firm some years before. Making blueprints was a new business in the 1890s, and Makepeace could see a future in it. Builders and architects needed blueprints, but they weren't easy to make in those days. Specially sensitized paper was needed and the paper had to be put under glass and rolled out into the sun to be exposed. After that it was hand-washed in a water and chemical bath to make the exposed part of the drawing on the blueprint turn blue.

After apprenticing for a time, Makepeace opened his own business on Washington Street. He chose the top floor because of its access to the sun. But since he wanted to be able to make blueprints at night as well as by day, he developed carbon arc lamps to illuminate the paper and reduce the required exposure time.

His business expanded, and soon he was coating his own blueprint paper. He bought a horse and wagon to deliver his blueprints. He also started selling drafting supplies and drawing implements.

By 1909, the business had outgrown its 345 Washington Street space; it moved many times in downtown Boston and into Back Bay and Cambridge. In 1946 Makepeace died and Stephen Joyce, the company's assistant treasurer and office manager, bought it from the heirs. In 1983, B.L. Makepeace Inc. moved to Brighton.

When Bernard Makepeace started his firm, a move to Brighton would have been outlandish, for then it was New England's major cattle market. Cows grazed on its green fields and market gardens and nurseries thrived. Today, however, Brighton is a center for much light industry and is the new home of Boston public radio station WGBH.

Makepeace has gone far beyond making blueprints and selling drafting and artists' supplies, although it does still offer surveying equipment, builders' tape and chalk, and hard hats, digital copiers, and plotters in a downstairs showroom. But its main claim to fame is as the oldest reprographer—reproducer of such graphic images as drawings, photographs, and paintings—in metropolitan Boston.

MSPCA-ANGELL

350 SOUTH HUNTINGTON AVENUE, BOSTON
☎ (617) 522-7400
🚇 MBTA GREEN LINE E TO HEATH STREET
TUESDAY-SATURDAY 11AM TO 4PM

✦

*R*EADING HIS NEWSPAPER ONE SPRING DAY IN 1868, BOSTON LAWYER GEORGE T. ANGELL was distressed to learn of the deaths of two horses from exhaustion. They had been raced more than forty miles over rough roads from Worcester to Brighton. Feeling that something should be done about such cruelty, he made his opinions known. He spoke around the city to such groups as the Coachmen's Benevolent Association, proposing that working horses, like people, should have one day off a week, and that horses' tails not be docked. Soon wealthy humanitarian Emily Appleton joined him in taking up the cause of injured, maltreated, and homeless animals.

Two years earlier, in New York, Henry Bergh had founded the American Society for the Prevention of Cruelty to Animals, which provided a model for Angell and Appleton. In less than a month, 1,300 residents of the Boston area joined Angell and Appleton in starting an animal protection organization.

Among its first board members were the governor, the lieutenant governor, and poet and essayist Ralph Waldo Emerson.

By the summer of 1868, the society was publishing a magazine, *Our Dumb Animals*, and the Massachusetts legislature had passed a law giving the newly created Massachusetts Society for the Prevention of Cruelty to Animals (MSPCA) stronger animal protection laws to work under than those in any other state.

A farmer who had been carrying calves to market tossed into an open wagon with their legs tied together started carrying them instead, untied, in an open wagon. He was asked why he had changed his habits and replied: "There's a law ag'in it," the first issue of *Our Dumb Animals* reported. Similarly, a drover from another state, who usually crammed the animals he planned to sell into a single railway cattle car, hired an additional car so the cattle would have more room when he got to the Massachusetts border because of the threat of proceedings against him if the animals were too crowded.

The MSPCA saw to it that drinking troughs for horses were placed around the city. It published the first American edition of British author Anna Sewell's *Black Beauty* and distributed it free of charge in Boston schools.

In 1915 the MSPCA opened Angell Memorial Hospital on Longwood Avenue for the treatment of animals and, in 1917, a shelter in Methuen to care for retired police horses. In 1924, a small animal adoption center was opened, also in Methuen. Today, the hospital and the adoption center stand side by side on South Huntington Avenue.

STODDARD'S

MALL AT CHESTNUT HILL,
199 BOYLSTON STREET, CHESTNUT HILL
☎ (617)244-4187
🚇 MBTA GREEN LINE D TO CHESTNUT HILL
MONDAY-FRIDAY 10AM TO 9:30PM;
SATURDAY UNTIL 8PM; SUNDAY 2 TO 6PM

✦

"YOU CAN SPEND $10,000 FOR A GOOD KNIFE WITHOUT MUCH DIFFICULTY," SAYS DAVID Marks, Stoddard's present owner. The store specializes in knives of all sorts. Besides hunting knives there are Victorinox Swiss Army knives, Wusthoff knives from Germany, Sheffield knives from England, and handmade Benti culinary knives from Italy.

For two centuries, the cutlery company that began as Dame, Stoddard and Kendall in 1800 occupied three sites in the heart of Boston before moving its entire operation to the suburbs in 2005. From its founding until 1965 it stood on Washington Street. Then, after urban renewal destroyed its original home, the cutlery store moved to a four-story building on Temple Place near Downtown Crossing, where it remained for thirty-nine years. In time, however, it also opened a subsidiary shop at Copley Place. Traffic congestion on little Temple Place, however, prompted the move of the main store to Chestnut Hill in 2004, where the company already had a suburban store. In 2004 its Copley Place store moved to Chestnut Hill as well. But plans are in place, its owner insists, to see that Stoddard's gets back into the heart of downtown where it was a city fixture for so long.

Not much is known about the early years of the company. In 1927, Hungarian-born Bernard Marcovitz, who had come to America as a child, went to work in Boston as a wholesale cutlery distributor. Dame, Stoddard and Kendall was one of his accounts. When it was up for sale in 1928 he bought it. For simplicity's sake, he reduced its name to Stoddard's.

Over time the company grew from its origins as a small retail store to a bigger operation, thanks to the ways its owner thought to diversify the business. On a buying trip to Sheffield, England, in the 1930s, Marcovitz learned that the manufacturer of Raleigh bicycles wanted to expand sales into America. So he imported Raleighs to Boston, assembling them on the second floor of the Washington Street store. Once a bicycle was put together, the mechanic would ride it to the buyer's home and take the trolley back.

Marcovitz saw nothing unusual in selling bicycles. After all, like good knives, Raleigh bicycles were steel, made well, and had a certain integrity.

When Bernard's son, Arthur (the family name, by then, had been shortened to Marks), a fly-fisherman as well as a salesman, entered the business, the company began offering fly-fishing trips to Maine on early Boston & Maine Airways DC10s. From its earliest days, Stoddard's had sold handmade fly rods and hands-tied flies, so the concept fit.

Today Stoddard's continues to sharpen scissors and knives and to sell the finest cutlery. Sir Winston Churchill, once seeking an appropriate gift while on a visit to Boston, sent an aide to Stoddard's to buy Sheffield steel knives.

David Marks, grandson of Bernard, no longer carries fly-fishing equipment, but besides the knives in the glass display cases there are compasses and clocks, telescopes, magnifying glasses, bottle openers, and manicure sets. And, of course, scissors: sewing scissors, egg-cutting scissors, and ceremonial ribbon-cutting shears.

As a reminder of the company's rich past, a giant-size knife, designed as a window advertisement in Bernard Marcovitz's day, fills a whole showcase by itself.

THE SWAN BOATS OF BOSTON

BOSTON PUBLIC GARDEN, BOSTON
☎ (617) 522-1966
🚊 MBTA GREEN LINE TO ARLINGTON
MID-APRIL TO JUNE 20 10AM TO 4PM; JUNE 21
TO LABOR DAY 10AM TO 5PM; LABOR DAY TO
LATE SEPTEMBER MONDAY-FRIDAY NOON TO 4PM;
SATURDAY, SUNDAY 10AM TO 4PM

✦

SINCE 1877, IN THE WARM MONTHS, THE SWAN BOATS OF BOSTON HAVE GLIDED ON THE STILL waters of the Public Garden's three- and three-quarter-acre lagoon, carrying wide-eyed children and nostalgic adults. They have passed under the little iron suspension footbridge, rounded the lagoon's mini-island, passed dipping mallards, and left the "real" world behind for a quarter of an hour.

Robert Paget, a Northern Irishman employed at the Charlestown Navy Yard, conceived the idea of a catamaran with a paddlewheel in the stern that could be pedaled bicycle-fashion. The boats he built seated eight, and the pedaling apparatus was concealed beneath a giant white-painted copper swan. His inspiration was Richard Wagner's *Lohengrin*, an opera he loved. In it, the knight Lohengrin crosses a river in a boat drawn by a swan.

Although Paget died just a year after inventing his swan boats, his widow continued the business of renting them out at the Public Garden. Later his son John enlarged the boats so they could carry twenty passengers apiece. Today Lynn Paget, a great-granddaughter of the inventor, owns the six boats in the graceful fleet. In season, they are anchored off their own dock, within sight of Boylston Street in the garden. There, passengers climb aboard to be pedaled about. In winter, the boats are dismantled and stored.

In Brief

BILTMORE-GREEN LUGGAGE, 176 BOYLSTON STREET, BOSTON. In 1908, Ludwig Green opened four luggage stores in the city—on Canal, Washington, Charles, and Boylston Streets. The latter, selling wallets, passport folders, attachés, briefcases, flasks, and travel alarms as well as luggage, is the only one that remains. Situated in the theater district, its customers have included actors and actresses. Among them was Katherine Hepburn, who purchased two alarm clocks to ensure that she would make it to the theater on time. The day after her purchase, however, she returned the louder one.

CHELSEA CLOCK, 284 EVERETT AVENUE, CHELSEA. Designer of automobile clocks, U.S. Navy clocks, White House clocks, striking ship's bell clocks, and airplane clocks among others, Chelsea Clock was founded in 1897 in Chelsea. Today, Chelsea Clocks are widely sold in many gift and nautical stores, but historic Chelsea Clocks are repaired only at this Chelsea Clock factory.

NEW ENGLAND FLAG AND BANNER, 87 BEAVER STREET, WALTHAM. Since 1892, when this company started as New England Decorating in downtown Boston, it has hand-sewn flags for parades, hotels, embassies, yacht clubs, corporations, colleges, sports teams, and individuals. Customers have included, among others, Harvard and Boston Universities for their championship teams, the Boston Celtics basketball team, and the Boston Bruins hockey team. The store is open by appointment.

ROBERT E. WHITE INSTRUMENTS, INC., 711 ATLANTIC AVENUE, BOSTON. In 1918, Wilfred O. White opened the nautical instrument shop on State Street that later moved to Commercial Wharf and is now on Atlantic Avenue. But long before that, in 1875, Wilfred White's father-in-law, Captain George W. Eldridge, published the first annual *Eldridge Tide and Pilot Book*, a guide to East Coast waters. George W. was not, however, the first in his family to be concerned with matters of time and tide. His father, George Eldridge of Chatham, Massachusetts, in 1854 had published *Eldridge's Pilot for Vineyard Sound and Monomoy Shoals*. That was followed by publication of his charts of the area.

It was because young George W. was going from schooner to schooner in the busy harbor of Vineyard Haven, selling his father's charts and book to the schooner captains waiting for the right current to set sail, that he had the idea of making a current table for those going beyond Vineyard Sound waters. This became the tide and pilot book.

RESTAURANTS

✦

[167]

AMRHEIN'S RESTAURANT

80 WEST BROADWAY, SOUTH BOSTON
☎ (617) 268-6189
🚇 MBTA RED LINE TO BROADWAY
MONDAY-THURSDAY 11:30AM TO 10PM; FRIDAY,
SATURDAY TO 11PM; SUNDAY 10AM TO 9PM

✦

*W*HEN ADAM SEBASTIAN AMRHEIN ARRIVED IN BOSTON FROM GERMANY IN THE 1870s, Boston's German population was sizable enough to warrant his opening a good German bakery. By 1879 he was in business in the South End with a bread store on Shawmut Avenue and another enterprise on Oneida Street. By 1892 his bakery had become the Adam Amrhein Coffee Tavern located in this red-brick building in South Boston. About a half a mile away was the waterfront crammed with shipyards, machine shops, and refineries and their hard-working, hungry workers. Since the 1840s, South Boston had also been a popular settling place for Irish immigrants fleeing the potato famine.

Amrhein's, however, was especially popular in those early days for its hearty German food. Pigs' knuckles, pigs' feet, and wiener schnitzel were standbys on the menu. But when Amrhein's son, Adam Jacob, in 1907 married Ellen Ryan, who was from

[168]

an Irish immigrant family, he recognized the newly arrived Irish as an untapped market. By then, he also had a partner, F.R. Reiser.

It wasn't long before corned beef and cabbage had been added to the menu and the bar at Amrhein's and Reiser's was being kept busy by Irish patrons who came early and stayed late as they had at their local pubs in the Old Country. The bar to which they gravitated wasn't an ordinary bar. Said to be the oldest hand-carved bar in America, it is made of mahogany and extends twelve feet along one wall with a mirror behind it. Devils, griffins, and a fruit basket are among the carved embellishments. Since beer was one of the favorite libations of its Irish customers, Amrhein's installed a pump to draw draft out of the barrels. Today that pump is prominently displayed in a glass case just inside the door.

Amrhein's (the partner didn't last very long) became a much-frequented watering place for the city's Irish-American politicians, four-time mayor of Boston James Michael Curley among them. In an earlier era, King Camp Gillette, inventor of the Gillette Safety Razor, who had established his plant a block away, is said to have liked to have his lunch at Amrhein's. By 1954, Guy (Buster) Amrhein, one of Adam Jacob's five children, had taken over what, by then, was being called Amrhein's Restaurant.

Today, in the restaurant's dark wood-paneled Curley Room, adorned with photos of James Michael Curley, it isn't at all difficult to imagine political deals being made over a pint or two of draft beer and a hearty lunch.

Meanwhile, longshoreman Joseph Mulrey opened Mul's Diner in 1961 on the other side of West Broadway. In 1967, he bought Amrhein's, too, along with the Amrhein Family Wine Store, which Adam Jacob owned next door.

Joe Mulrey's son Stephen and grandson Rory have refurbished the pub to bring it up with the times, although they still serve plenty of meat and potatoes and pints of beer. And, nowadays, in addition to the politicos who come for lunch, a younger, more sophisticated set frequents the bar at night.

CAFÉ MARLIAVE

10 BOSWORTH STREET, BOSTON
☎ (617) 423-6340
🚋 MBTA RED OR GREEN LINE TO PARK STREET;
GREEN OR BLUE LINE TO GOVERNMENT CENTER
MONDAY-SATURDAY 11AM TO 5PM

✦

*H*ISTORY VIRTUALLY HOVERS IN THE AIR AROUND CAFÉ MARLIAVE. IN THE SEVEN-teenth century, Province House, the seat of the royal governors, was sited here. A spacious garden surrounded that mansion, and it is believed that the granite steps with the wrought iron arch that lead up to Café Marliave were once a part of its grounds.

In the nineteenth century, Paul Revere was interred in the Granary Burying Ground just at the top of little Bosworth Street on which the café fronts. There he joined Revolutionary leaders John Hancock and Samuel Adams and, one legend has it, Mother Goose of nursery rhyme fame.

Café Marliave was first situated on nearby Tremont Street, flourishing in close proximity to the golden-domed New State House designed by Charles Bulfinch in 1798. Bulfinch was in much demand as an architect at the time, and was the designer of many of Boston's public buildings and loveliest mansions. The State House was his most famous early work. After Café Marliave was destroyed by fire, its owner, Henri Marliave, a native of France, rebuilt it here at the foot of little Bosworth Street in 1878.

Among those frequenting it in those days was the Irish poet and anti-English activist John Boyle O'Reilly. In a corner booth, above which his picture now hangs, O'Reilly would regale his dining companions with the story of his escape from the penal colony in Australia to which he had been sent for seditious activities in Ireland. And he would recount how, once in Boston, he and fellow Fenians had helped arrange the escape on a New Bedford whaling ship of six more Fenians who had been sent to Australia.

Henri Marliave kept the restaurant into the early years of the twentieth century. Some say it was he who introduced *table d'hôte* (today's *prix fixe*) dining to the city of Boston. His nephew, Charles, ran the restaurant until 1935, when Albert Amedei and Antonio Rosetti bought the establishment. The two had worked together—Amedei as chef and Rosetti as waiter—in a Tremont Street restaurant. They set to work refurbishing the restaurant, decorating its walls with the *fleurs-de-lis* of France and incorporating an "M" for Marliave into the design of the mosaic floor.

In 1965, Rosetti's son, Roy, took over and remained its owner until 1994. Today, Frank Iacoviello, who was nurtured in the food business in the city's Italian North End, and a partner, Jean Bruno, own it. Although the restaurant now serves Southern Italian fare, the *fleurs-de-lis* on the pressed tin walls and the mosaic floor remain.

DOYLE'S

3484 WASHINGTON STREET, JAMAICA PLAIN

☎ (617)524-2345

🚇 MBTA ORANGE LINE TO GREEN STREET

DAILY 9AM TO 1AM

✦

*A*NY BOSTON POLITICIAN WORTH HIS SALT HAS HAD A DRINK NOW AND AGAIN AT DOYLE'S. There's a James Michael Curley Table, named after the popular mayor who was a regular for Doyle's corned beef and cabbage and a pint of good brew. (Curley lived nearby in a house with shamrocks on the shutters.) There's a John F. "Honey Fitz" Fitzgerald Room, honoring the first Irish-American to become mayor, in 1905, of Boston. A Mayors' Table honors Kevin White, Thomas Menino, and Raymond Flynn, and there's a Thomas Menino Room, too. (At Doyle's, regulars like to gossip about the time Mayor Flynn and President Bill Clinton had lunch at Doyle's and how, by the time the meal was over, Flynn had been named ambassador to the Vatican.)

But Doyle's didn't start out as a neighborhood bar/restaurant. When, in 1882, Dennis Doyle, from Ireland's County Roscommon, opened his business on Washington Street, it was a general store, saloon, and prize-fighting ring under one roof. In those days Jamaica Plain abounded in breweries, as a brook there provided clear, sparkling water for beer making. Anyone who went walking in the neighborhood got whiffs of the brewers' hops and malt. And those who stopped in at Doyle's might see Heavyweight Champion of the World, Roxbury-born John L. Sullivan—whose mother came from County Roscommon, too—doing a little fighting in the ring near the bar.

In 1900, Dennis died, but the saloon stayed in family hands. In 1907, in order to protect Stony Brook, the precious source of brewery water, a culvert was built to cap it, and Doyle's had to be moved to make way. The saloon was put up on rollers, and a horse and team hauled it to its present site.

During Prohibition, Doyle's stayed open as a speakeasy, although its neighbor, Burke's Tavern, on the corner of Washington Street and Rossmore Road, was forced to close down. That didn't bother owner Billy Burke, though. He turned bootlegger and supplied Doyle's.

Today, Doyle's is owned by the Burkes—Billy Burke's son, Gerry, Gerry's son Gerry Jr., and his nephew Chris Spellman. The 1890s tin ceiling is still above the forty-eight-foot mahogany-topped bar, along with paintings of Blarney Castle and a sailing ship on the high seas. Murals of Kilkenny Castle, Plymouth Rock, Boston's Old and New State Houses, Paul Revere's ride, and, incongruously, Switzerland's Lake Geneva, decorate the café walls. Of course a photograph of John L. Sullivan, Heavy Weight Champion of the World from 1882 to 1892, is displayed, too.

DURGIN-PARK MARKET
DINING ROOMS

340 FANEUIL HALL MARKET PLACE, BOSTON

☎ (617) 227-2038

🚇 MBTA GREEN OR ORANGE LINES TO
HAYMARKET; OR BLUE LINE TO AQUARIUM
MONDAY-SATURDAY 11:30AM TO 10PM;
SUNDAY 11AM TO 9PM

✦

*I*F PETER FANEUIL, BACK IN THE 1730S,
HADN'T AGREED TO REMAIN A BACHELOR,
Boston, down through the centuries, would have had
no Faneuil Hall, no Faneuil Hall Marketplace, and
no Durgin-Park. But the wily young merchant ac-
quiesced when his wealthy ship- and wharf-owning
uncle, French-born Andrew Faneuil, requested that
he not marry. Peter's brother, Benjamin, who was
the heir apparent and of whom the same request
was made, did not follow his uncle's wishes and was
virtually disinherited. It is said that their uncle's an-
tagonism to marriage was the result of his own un-
happiness after his wife died.

In exchange for remaining a bachelor, Peter
Faneuil received his uncle's Tremont Street mansion and property elsewhere in New England, as well
as in England, France, and Holland. All this made

him Boston's wealthiest resident in his day.

Bachelor he might have been, but Peter enjoyed good company and was not at all averse to having a good time. Indeed, it is said that he was something of a bon vivant and thoroughly enjoyed entertaining. It is precisely because he liked good food and drink and couldn't readily find what he wanted that he offered to give a central market to Boston.

In those days, the food sellers sold their produce from carts all around town. Faneuil proposed to bring them together under one roof, in a building he would provide. Many merchants feared this would reduce their sales and so were opposed to a public market house. In the end, however, Boston accepted Faneuil's offer. Since 1742, Faneuil Hall Market has been a centerpiece of this historic city.

But it has undergone many changes over the years. Only Faneuil Hall's brick walls and its copper grasshopper weathervane survived a ferocious fire in 1761. By this time, Bostonians were so fond of the hall that they held a public lottery to pay to have it rebuilt; it reopened in 1763. On its second floor, which, for twenty years had been the site of town meetings, there now began to be revolutionary activities. Indeed, these are said to have led General Lafayette, in 1824, when he returned to Boston after the Revolution, to single out Faneuil Hall, along with Boston in general, to be dubbed "The Cradle of Liberty." In 1805, Boston architect Charles Bulfinch renovated and enlarged the building, doubling its width and adding a third story.

Then in 1826, under Mayor Josiah Quincy, three new long white granite market structures, consisting of a central meat market and two adjacent storage areas called the North and South Market Buildings, all designed by Alexander Parris, were erected behind Faneuil Hall. They were called Quincy Market in honor of the mayor. Today, Quincy Market's three buildings are known as Faneuil Hall Marketplace while Faneuil Hall keeps its original name. The marketplace buildings are now the site of souvenir and food shops. Faneuil Hall itself, as it has since Peter Faneuil's day, serves the people of Boston in various ways. New citizens are sworn in and political debates held on its second floor. The League of Women Voters meets there, while on its ground floor are shop concessions and an information center.

In the old days, however, on the second floor of the North Market Building, dining rooms for the hard-working market men and weary sailors who frequented the area were opened. Before long, Eldridge Park, owner of a neighboring livery stable; John Durgin, who came of a restaurant-owning family; and John Chandler, a dry goods merchant, bought the dining rooms, giving them the name Durgin-Park. Although both Durgin and Park died within two years, Chandler retained the name. When he found that shoppers enjoyed rubbing elbows with market workers, he enlarged the restaurant. For more than sixty-five years, the Chandler family ran Durgin-Park. Then James Hallett, a market worker, bought it from Chandler. Since 1976, the families of Martin Kelley and Michael Solimando have been its owners.

The food at Durgin-Park has always been hearty, stick-to-the-ribs Yankee fare. Pot roast, prime ribs, fishcakes, baked beans, roast turkey, codfish, corn bread, and Indian pudding are perennial favorites. (Calvin Coolidge is said to have favored the cod.) For years, the food was served home style on long tables for twenty topped with red- and white-checked tablecloths, and the waitresses were renowned for being surly.

Today there are tables for two and four that look down on the marketplace. It is no longer the marketplace of the past, however, for in the years that followed World War II, the wholesale market was moved out of town. The stalls that remained became dingy and unattractive, so, in the 1970s, Rowse and Company of Columbia, Maryland, revamped and leased them. They are now leased by the city of

Boston to a Chicago company. In the white granite Quincy Market buildings once crowded with produce, T-shirts and Boston Red Sox souvenirs are sold, and fast food eateries abound. As for old-fashioned produce stalls, on Fridays and Saturday mornings vendors hawk their vegetables and fruit, and butchers and fishmongers sell indoors at the Haymarket across the street from Faneuil Hall.

Through it all, venerable Durgin-Park of the red- and white-checked tablecloths has held its own. Its waitresses are known for always remembering the names and the favorite dishes of longtime customers—and for their casual sassiness.

LOCKE-OBER

3 WINTER PLACE, BOSTON

☎ (617) 542-1340

🚇 MBTA RED LINE TO PARK STREET

MONDAY-FRIDAY 11:30AM TO 2:30PM AND 5:30 TO
10PM; FRIDAY TO 11PM; SATURDAY 5:30 TO 10PM

✦

*H*ALF A BLOCK FROM THE BOSTON COMMON, DOWN THE LITTLE ALLEY KNOWN AS WINter Place, is Locke-Ober's, a destination of the city's discriminating diners for generations. Time was when there were houses on Winter Place—and, in the cellar of one of them, in 1859, a French Alsatian, Louis Ober, opened a small café. By 1875, that cafe had been transformed into Ober's Restaurant Parisien at Three and Four Winter Place, advertised as serving "French cooking, par excellence."

Over time, the main restaurant moved up to the first floor, private dining rooms were opened on the second, and Louis Ober's family lived on the third. King's Dictionary of Boston was soon saying that Ober's cuisine was "unsurpassed in the city of Boston." By 1886, Ober was doing well enough to remodel. He bought Santo Domingo mahogany for the bar and imported woodcarvers from France to carve it. To devise a way to keep food warm, he

[182]

asked designers in Germany to develop metal steam dishes, fashioned with weights and counter weights to lift their covers, and had Reed and Barton, silversmiths, make the dishes for him.

Keeping only a small apartment on the third floor, Ober gave over the rest of the building to the business, turning the downstairs dining room into the men's bar. Since barroom paintings of nudes were then in vogue, he commissioned an Italian artist to paint one for him. Life couldn't have been better.

But in 1892, Frank Locke, a retired Maine sea captain, decided he would open a café at One and Two Winter Place. His was designed to outdo Louis Ober's. Locke's Wine Rooms were lined with mirrors of heavy plate and rich cut glass. As in Ober's, there was much polished mahogany. The bar rail was of embossed glass hollowed out so it could be filled with artificial roses. Damask hangings graced the walls while quilted and embossed satin covered the ceilings. A tumbling waterfall was also part of the décor. But those who came to Frank Locke's soon realized that the food next door at Ober's was vastly better. So they would stop at Locke's to drink, then move on to Ober's grand restaurant to eat. So common did it become for guests to drink in one establishment and eat in the other that a small door linked Locke's bar to Ober's dining room.

In 1894, the competition ended when Wood and Pollard, wholesale liquor dealers, bought both establishments, and the walls between the two were removed. Another Frenchman, Emil Camus, was made the manager of the new joint enterprise, which was renamed the Winter Place Tavern. There were several more changes in ownership until, in 1898, the establishment was renamed the Locke-Ober Company.

Unlike Ober, Camus did not wish his restaurant to be a French restaurant only; he wanted to offer the best culinary fare of all nations. And so, while the menu included such dishes as Filet Mignon Mirabeau and Sweetbreads Eugenie, diners could also choose to have a New England Boiled Dinner, Lobster Savannah, or Baked Oysters Winter Place.

In 1919, with Prohibition arrived, the Locke side of the establishment was closed, and the restaurant, without the bar, had to survive on the quality of its fine food and service. Clearly, it did: *The Boston Evening Transcript* in 1930 called the restaurant Boston's "high and holy temple of fine living." But all of this was for men only. Not until 1971 could women eat anywhere but in the third floor dining rooms at Lock-Ober's.

Today, what was once Louis Ober's barroom is Locke-Ober's main dining room. Although the Reed and Barton steam dishes had been sold, they have been repurchased and stand again on the bar. The nude continues to smile from the wall. Nowadays there are touches of the Orient in the dishes served, along with New England cuisine. Since 2001, Boston chef Lydia Shire and Paul Licari have been the owners, with Lydia Shire adding her own very personal modern touches to this historic Boston restaurant.

UNION OYSTER HOUSE

41 UNION STREET, BOSTON

☎ (617) 227-2750

🚇 MBTA ORANGE OR GREEN LINES TO HAYMARKET

SUNDAY-THURSDAY 11AM TO 9PM;

FRIDAY, SATURDAY 11AM TO 10PM

✦

*I*N THE SEVENTEENTH AND EIGHTEENTH CEN-
TURIES, UNION STREET WAS THE HEART OF
Boston. The harbor waters lapped at the back doors
of the sailmakers, ropemakers, boat builders, and
chandlers who plied their trades along the stone-
paved street. Ships lay alongside the wharfs, crowded with seamen and passersby, unloading everything
from Chinese firecrackers to carved ivories. In 1742
the building located at Number 41, known as "At the
Sign of the Cornfields," was the Hopestill Capen silk
and fancy dress goods shop. The waterfront location
of this brick-and-wood three-story structure was
ideal for receiving deliveries of fine cloth from ships
arriving from Europe.

In 1826 the fancy dress goods shop was transformed into the Atwood and Bacon Oyster House by
Hawes Atwood and Allen Holbrook Bacon, who installed its trademark semi-circular mahogany oyster
bar. It was at this bar that lawyer-orator Daniel Web-

ster washed down his oysters on the half shell with tumblers of brandy and water. Legend has it that he regularly consumed six platefuls—with half a dozen oysters on each plate. In those days the oysters could be served roasted or stewed as well as on the half shell, and scallops and clams were also popular. If customers weren't in the mood for seafood, they could order crackers and milk, a dropped egg, milk toast, or squash or custard pie.

As they enjoyed their meals, diners could reflect on the historical pedigree of the building. Earlier, in 1771, on the eve of the American Revolution, the seditious publication *The Massachusetts Spy* was printed upstairs. Its publisher, Isaiah Thomas, just managed to get his press onto a boat and carried across to Charlestown before the British raided. From Charlestown, Thomas transported his press to Worcester from where he was able to gleefully print the first report of the Battles of Lexington and Concord. During the Revolution itself, this house was the headquarters of the Continental Army paymaster, so troops came here to collect their wages.

In 1796, in the aftermath of the French Revolution, the exiled Duc de Chartres, who one day would be Louis Philippe, the King of France, took rooms here, paying his way by giving French lessons by the brick fireplace to the young ladies of Boston.

It is said that the first toothpicks in the nation were introduced at the Union Oyster House in 1869 by Charles Foster of Oxford City, Maine. He had seen natives using wooden toothpicks on a trip to South America, and decided to produce them as novelties. Oyster house proprietors at first turned down his proposal to try out the toothpicks at their establishment, but after Foster persuaded Harvard students to demand them, the restaurant had a change of heart.

In 1892, the Greaves family of Boston bought the oyster house, changing its name to the one it bears today. In 1970, Joseph Milano, a liquor and food dealer, entered a partnership with their heirs. Today, his children, Joseph Jr. and Marianne, are the owners.

Every July and August, 3,000 to 4,000 oysters a day are dispensed from the antique oyster bar, and sizable numbers—though not quite so many—in other seasons. These may be Gerrish Island oysters from Delaware; Malpeque oysters from Prince Edward Island, Canada; Island Creek oysters from Duxbury, Massachusetts; or Cotuit oysters from Cotuit, Massachusetts. And in the wooden booths upstairs and down, Bostonians and tourists alike dine on hot cornbread and steaming bowls of clam chowder, lobsters, scrod, Indian pudding, and gingerbread.

Presidents Franklin Delano Roosevelt and Bill Clinton have eaten at the Union Oyster House, which is said to be the nation's oldest continuing restaurant. And, from a booth at the top of the bare creaking wooden stairs, Jack Kennedy frequently ordered boiled lobster of a Sunday when he was in his hometown.

JACOB WIRTH RESTAURANT

31-37 STUART STREET, BOSTON
☎ (617) 338-8586
🚋 MBTA GREEN LINE TO BOYLSTON; OR
ORANGE LINE TO CHINATOWN OR NEW
ENGLAND MEDICAL CENTER
MONDAY-THURSDAY 11AM TO 10PM; FRIDAY,
SATURDAY TO MIDNIGHT; SUNDAY TO 8PM

✦

WHEN JACOB (JAKE) WIRTH OPENED HIS RES-
TAURANT SUPPLY BUSINESS IN DOWNTOWN
Boston in the 1860s, the neighborhood was bustling
with fellow German immigrants. Jake had come to
Boston from Kreuzebach near Bingen in Germany,
where his family had vineyards overlooking the
River Rhine. On Boston's Shawmut Avenue, just a
few streets away from where he settled, there was
a German Catholic church that served as a community center. Named the Church of the Holy Trinity,
it is still standing.

Wirth opened his supply company on Eliot
Street (then named Stuart Street, across from the
restaurant's present location). As his company prospered, it became clear to him that someone had to
feed the teamsters who were making his deliveries, so he opened this German restaurant in 1888. It

served such hearty Teutonic fare as pigs' knuckles, herring, sauerkraut, spaetzle, and sauerbraten along with the thirst-quenching brew the working men liked. Wirth also took advantage of his own heritage and began importing his family's Rhine Valley wines.

The building where Wirth first welcomed diners was one of a number of bow-front Greek Revival row houses that had been built in 1845. When his restaurant prospered, Wirth bought the building next door to enlarge his serving space. Today, these two buildings are the only survivors of their kind still standing in the neighborhood. The Wirths lived above the restaurant, and it was there that Jacob Wirth Jr. was born in 1880.

Young Jake grew up happily playing in his father's restaurant with its sawdust-covered floors and long dark mahogany bar with the motto *"Sum Cuique"* ("To Each his Own") carved above it. Although young Jake entered Harvard College in 1901, he was forced to drop out when he caught typhoid fever, and he never went back. Instead he took over management of the restaurant, which thrived even though, during the First World War, he could no longer import his family's wines.

Despite Prohibition and the anti-German sentiment of World Wars I and II, Jacob Wirth's never closed. During Prohibition, its tactic was to sell near beer (malt beverages containing little or no alcohol) brewed by the Haffenreffer Company in Boston's Jamaica Plain. Its 3.2% alcohol content was low enough to be acceptable. It was kept in kegs in the cellar, and a ramp led from the storage area right to the bar. At Jake Wirth's they still recount with amusement how John L. Sullivan, heavyweight boxing champion of the world in 1910, was in the way of one of the barrels as it rolled toward the bar, flattening Sullivan in a way no opponent ever had.

In the days of Jake Sr. and Jr., the restaurant's waiters were as German as most of the fare. One of them, Frederick (Fritz) Fruth, who worked at Jake Wirth's from 1875 to 1951, liked reminiscing about its patrons and how he frequently knew three generations of the same family.

Representatives of those families from all walks of life attended Jake Jr.'s 85th birthday party in 1964. Poet David McCord wrote a ballad for the occasion, while the dean of the Harvard Graduate School of Arts and Sciences offered birthday greetings in Latin. Jake Jr. died a year later.

His widow ran the restaurant until 1975, when one of its frequenters, William Fitzgerald, who owned the parking lot next door, bought it. Today his son Kevin is its owner.

Jake Wirth's is still much as it has been from the beginning, with creaking dark plank floors (sawdust-covered until a fire broke out in the sawdust), high ceilings, bare dark wooden tables, and bentwood chairs. Thirty kinds of beer are on tap and an additional twenty brands are sold in bottles.

The menu still offers German potato salad, sauerkraut, and wurst, but for more sophisticated palates, such dishes as baked cod with ginger or orange-glazed salmon are also offered.

In Brief

J.J. DONOVAN'S TAVERN, 27 CLINTON STREET, BOSTON. Although the history of the earliest years of this tavern on the ground floor below the Durgin-Park Restaurant is unclear, it was bought in 1912 by John J. Donovan and has remained in the family ever since. Until the 1940s, J.J. Donovan's was for men only, frequented primarily by the meat and produce workers of the market. It survived Prohibition by selling sandwiches rather than beer, then returned to its identity as a tavern when Prohibition was repealed. The original sawdust-covered floors remain. J.J. Donovan's and Durgin-Park are the only privately owned enterprises in the Faneuil Hall Marketplace today.

INNS & HOTELS

✦

THE COLLEGE CLUB OF BOSTON

44 COMMONWEALTH AVENUE, BOSTON

☎ (617) 536-9510

🚇 MBTA GREEN LINE TO ARLINGTON

✦

SHORTLY BEFORE CHRISTMAS IN 1880, NINE
TEEN COLLEGE ALUMNAE MET OVER TEA TO
discuss establishing a club "for sociability and companionship" for college women "among their kind"
in Boston. The club, they decided, would sponsor social events and offer lectures, and, indeed, among its
noted guests in those early years would be the writers Mark Twain, Frances Hodgson Burnett, and Oliver Wendell Holmes, who considered Boston "the
thinking center of the continent, and therefore of
the planet."

The club had various locations in those early
days, but in 1905 it was able to buy a home of its
own at 40 Commonwealth Avenue. There it offered
members seven "sleeping rooms" and a drawing
room as well as a meeting room. The membership
fee went from $10 to $15 annually. Between 1910
and 1992, with a combination of membership money and contributions from wealthy members, the
club purchased several houses along Commonwealth
Avenue. All but its present home, at 44 Common

wealth, have since been sold. Today's club, acquired in 1925, is in a Victorian brownstone with a slate mansard roof.

Inside the four-story house are a sweeping staircase, high ceilings, marble floors on the first level, and the dark wood trim popular in High Victorian days. Then, as now, the rooms were decorated in college colors: with crimson rambler wallpaper for the Radcliffe Room; blue silk curtains in the Wellesley Room; a cherry and white décor for Boston University, and a white décor, with brass beds, for Smith. The Women's College Club, the oldest of its kind in the nation, continues to offer eleven rooms, not only to members but also to others seeking a bed and breakfast in Boston. As it always has, the club also offers cultural programs—often literary—to its members. Among events on its program in the last year have been a lecture by George Howe Colt, author of *The Big House*, about the family cottage on Cape Cod, and a visit to the 1804 Charles Bulfinch-designed Nichols House Museum on Beacon Hill.

THE COLONIAL INN

48 MONUMENT SQUARE, CONCORD

☎ (978) 369-9200

🚆 COMMUTER RAIL FROM NORTH STATION

✦

*T*HE STRUCTURES THAT MAKE UP THE CO-
LONIAL INN HAVE STOOD IN THE CENTER OF
Concord for almost three centuries. In 1775, legend
has it, they, like other places in town, served as storage places for the Minute Men's arms and provisions.

Two decades after the Minute Men fought the
British, Boston merchant John Thoreau purchased
the house that is now the right-hand part of the inn.
The other two structures have also, over time, been
assimilated into today's inn. John Thoreau's two
daughters inherited their father's house, and during
the years he was attending Harvard, Henry David,
their nephew, was a frequent guest. In time, their
home became the Thoreau House Hotel. One of the
other original structures was turned into a general
store, while the third remained a residence for years.
The whole finally became the Colonial in 1898 and
began to be called an inn in the early 1900s.

Over the years, the fifty-six-room gray-clap-
board Colonial Inn has passed through many hands.
Today's owners are German-born hotelier Jurgen

Demisch and his wife, Rebecca, who have refurbished its rooms in colonial style. The inn's two dining rooms, open daily for lunch and dinner, serve traditional Yankee fare such as chicken potpie, cornbread, Indian pudding, and clam chowder.

LONGFELLOW'S WAYSIDE INN

72 WAYSIDE INN ROAD, SUDBURY

☎ (978) 443-1776

🚗 MASS TURNPIKE TO 128 NORTH, EXIT 26 TO
ROUTE 20 WEST, 11 MILES TO WAYSIDE INN ROAD.
🚃 COMMUTER RAIL FROM SOUTH STATION TO
FRAMINGHAM, TAXI EIGHT MILES TO
WAYSIDE INN ROAD.

✦

A HOSTELRY HAS STOOD ON THIS SYLVAN
SITE SINCE 1716. IN THE EIGHTEENTH AND
nineteenth centuries, stagecoaches from Worcester
and Boston trundled along the old Boston Post Road,
their drivers often stopping here to water their horses and to offer their passengers respite at the inn.
The building at the time it began to take in guests
was typical, but small by our standards—just four
rooms, two over two.

In its earliest days, the Wayside Inn was called
David How's Tavern. It was passed down to How's
son Ezekiel, a Minute Man who, on April 19, 1775,
led troops against the English. Upon Ezekiel death,
the hostelry was inherited by his son, and upon his
death, to his grandchildren, Joshua and Lyman.

In 1862, the year after Lyman Howe's death
(the "e" was added to the name in his lifetime),

poet Henry Wadsworth Longfellow stopped at the inn, which by then had fallen on hard times. Lyman had died in debt, and the surrounding land was being leased to tenant farmers who used the inn as a boarding house. With Longfellow's visit, however, the name and the fate of the old hostelry changed forever.

Despite its condition, the poet was inspired by what he saw and wrote:

> *One Autumn night in Sudbury town,*
> *Across the meadows bare and brown,*
> *The windows of the wayside inn*
> *Gleamed red with fire-light through the leaves*
> *Of woodbine hanging from the eaves*
> *Their crimson curtains rent and thin.*

Longfellow went on to write, in the book that he was to call *Tales of a Wayside Inn*, one of his most famous poems, "The Landlord's Tale: Paul Revere's Ride." The 1863 publication of Longfellow's book gradually stirred interest in the old inn, and in 1897, Edward R. Lemon of Malden, a wealthy wool merchant, bought and restored it.

Three years after Lemon's death in 1919, automobile magnate Henry Ford purchased the inn. In addition to renovating the hostelry itself, Ford established three schools, two for the children of his employees and one for underprivileged boys. He also built a gristmill, country store, and chapel on the grounds. On the night of December 21, 1955, the historic inn burned to the ground. It took three years to rebuild it, and when the reconstruction was done, the National Trust for Historic Preservation became the stewards of the inn property. They passed it on to a private trust controlled by Boston archivists and museum curators in the late 1960s.

Today, the Wayside Inn has museum-quality rooms for ten overnight guests that reflect the way the building looked 200 years ago, and a dining room that serves such traditional New England fare as pot roast, chicken pie, and fish cakes. The eighteenth-century innkeeper's room and the old kitchen, which both survived the fire, are still in use.

The private trust now managing the inn also manages the Wayside Inn Archives, which contain over half a million documents relating to the family and the Inn. It includes photographs, news clippings, menus, and other items going back to 1686. The Archives, which are on the grounds, are open by appointment only.

OMNI PARKER HOUSE

60 SCHOOL STREET, BOSTON
☎ (617) 227-8600
🚇 MBTA RED LINE TO PARK STREET; OR
GREEN LINE TO GOVERNMENT CENTER

✦

*O*PENING IN 1855, THE OMNI PARKER IS THE
OLDEST CONTINUOUSLY OPERATING HOTEL
in the nation. But the hotel has other, equally im-
pressive, claims to fame. Charles Dickens first read
A Christmas Carol to an American audience here,
and here Henry Wadsworth Longfellow wrote his
first draft of "Paul Revere's Ride." It was in the
Parker House library that John Greenleaf Whittier,
Ralph Waldo Emerson, Nathaniel Hawthorne, and
Francis Parkman met monthly on Saturday after-
noons to read their works and talk of bookish things.
And actor John Wilkes Booth, whose brother, Edwin,
was performing in Boston at the time, was a guest
at the Parker House in April, 1865. Seven days after
checking out, he went south to Washington, where
he assassinated President Abraham Lincoln.

In colonial times, School Street was a simple
thoroughfare of shops and stables, churches, and
little houses. Yet a grand brick mansion stood on the
site of what became the Parker House. By the 1800s,

the mansion had become an undistinguished boarding house.

Harvey D. Parker, a farm boy from Paris, Maine, arrived in Boston in 1825 with less than $1 in his satchel and found work as a coachman for a Watertown woman. Parker managed to buy a small café near School Street with his earnings and, in 1854, purchased the dilapidated mansion-turned-boarding house and demolished it. In its stead he had a marble-faced hotel constructed. Because his chateau-like hostelry rose five stories and cut off light to old historic King's Chapel behind it, legend has it that Parker installed Waterford crystal chandeliers in the chapel to compensate for natural light. Parker died in 1884.

Of the hotel, Hawthorne, who was taken with the extent of the alcoholic beverages that were offered, wrote that the most remarkable thing about it was the perfect order that prevailed.

It was for diners at the Parker House that the soft, folded roll that came to be known as the Parker House roll was created, as well as Boston cream pie with its chocolate frosting and yellow custard filling. (Among the hotel's pastry chefs from 1911 to 1913 was Ho Chi Minh, who later became the president of North Vietnam.)

Just as famous as the Parker House kitchen was

its dining room. In 1954, John F. Kennedy chose the Parker House dining room for the bachelor dinner before his wedding. And it is said that he asked Jacqueline Bouvier to marry him at Table Forty in the dining room.

There have been many changes in the Parker House since those early days. In 1927, all but one wing of the original hotel was demolished, which has allowed it to be described as "continuously operating," and a fourteen-story polished Quincy granite building replaced it. Since 1996, this has been an Omni Hotel property and there has been a complete renovation.

As the building has been brought up to date, so, rather sadly for old-time Bostonians, has the fare in the kitchen. Almonds are now sprinkled on the frosting of the Boston cream pie and the trademark fold has disappeared from the Parker House roll. About it, a popular limerick was once written.

> *A corpulent lady named Kroll*
> *Had an idea exceedingly droll.*
> *She went to a ball*
> *Dressed in nothing at all*
> *And backed in as a Parker House roll.*

YOUNG MEN'S
CHRISTIAN ASSOCIATION

(YMCA of Greater Boston)

316 HUNTINGTON AVENUE, BOSTON

☎ (617) 536-6950

🚊 MBTA GREEN LINE TO NORTHEASTERN

✦

*B*OSTON-BORN THOMAS VALENTINE SULLIVAN SHIPPED OUT IN 1819, WHEN HE WAS NINE-teen, on a sealing expedition in Antarctic waters. By the age of twenty-seven, in 1827, he had his first command, and two years later he owned three ships. But the seafaring life was a grueling one, and in the mid-1830s, having suffered shipwrecks and other adversities, Sullivan had a religious conversion and gave up the mariner's life.

At first he found his calling in ministering to boatmen on the Great Lakes, but in the 1840s he returned to Boston and began preaching and distrib-uting religious tracts on ships in the harbor. In 1851, he learned about the Young Men's Christian Asso-ciation that had been founded in London to provide Christian fellowship to young men newly arrived in that city.

A letter on the subject, written by George Van Derlip, a student from New York who had been studying in London, appeared in a Boston Baptist weekly. How wonderful such a club would be for the young sailors and immigrants who were alone in Boston, Sullivan felt. So he went to the leaders of the city's Protestant churches to ask for their assistance in starting a club.

He was enthusiastically received and before long had the backing of a number of Boston businessmen as well as of Methodist, Baptist, Congregational, and Episcopal leaders. Space was rented for Sullivan's proposed club in a building on Washington Street, and in March 1852 it had its gala opening with more than 600 men attending, Soon the young men who before had had only the city's dark streets, taverns, and brothels to welcome them could avail themselves of comfortable rooms filled with books, newspapers, and cozy chairs. Bible study was offered for those who wished it, and there were evening classes in such subjects as automotive repair and typing. Refreshments were served. Above all there was warmth and comradeship, and, eventually, simple accommodations available, too. The evening classes the YMCA offered evolved to become Northeastern University.

Over the years, the Y moved many times, but since the early twentieth century it has been housed in this gold brick Italian Renaissance building on

Huntington Avenue near Northeastern University. Its floors are of elegant marble, and mahogany balconies grace the spacious lobby. In winter it offers simple, basic rooms for men; from June through August, when the city tends to fill with young travelers, accommodations are available for both men and women. There is a gym and swimming pool plus a cafeteria for breakfasts and lunches.

In Brief

COPLEY SQUARE HOTEL, 47 HUNTINGTON AVENUE, BOSTON. Opened in 1891, Copley Square Hotel was for years the site of the Storyville Jazz Club as well as home to the popular Hungarian restaurant, Café Budapest. It was here that William McKinley had his Boston presidential campaign headquarters in 1896.

THE LENOX, 61 EXETER STREET, BOSTON. When Lucius Boomer, the president and managing director of New York City's Waldorf-Astoria, opened this hotel in 1900, it was hailed as "the Waldorf-Astoria of Boston," with its exterior of red and white terra cotta bricks and an interior more sumptuously decorated than that of any other hotel in the city. At eleven stories, it was also the tallest building in the

Back Bay at that time. Seven years later, opera singer Enrico Caruso arrived at the hotel in his private railroad car. In 1965, Judy Garland made the Lenox her home for three months.

INDEX

[210]

[211]

INDEX BY LOCATION

CAMBRIDGE
Dickson Bros. Co. · 100
Harvard Coop · 48
Keezer's · 51
La Flamme's Barber Shop of Harvard Square · 26
Leavitt & Peirce · 142
Masse Hardware · 102
Roach's Sporting Goods · 131
Schoenhof's Foreign Books · 37

CHARLESTOWN
Acme Bookbinding · 40

CHESTNUT HILL
Stoddard's · 160

CONCORD
The Colonial Inn · 198
Vanderhoof Hardware Company · 105

DORCHESTER
Deveney & White Monument Company · 138

HOLLISTON
James F. Fiske's General Store · 58

JAMAICA PLAIN
Doyle's · 174

ACKNOWLEDGEMENTS

*T*HE AUTHOR IS INDEBTED TO THE FOLLOW-
ING FOR THEIR GENEROUS PARTICIPATION:
Daphne Abeel and David Masse (Masse Hardware),
Brian Adams (MSPCA-Angell), Tom Adams, Mau-
reen Collins and Michael Thomas (Animal Rescue
League of Boston), Virgil Aiello (DeLuca's Market),
Ellen, Nancy, Mary F., J. Christopher, and Leo F. Am-
rhein Jr., Arthur Cote and Rory Mulrey (Amrhein's
Restaurant), James F. Brine (James F. Brine Inc.). Ross
Bellar (Simpson's Inc.), John Blacker (Morse Fish
Company), Larry and Joseph Bornstein and Jose-
phine Greene (Olympia Flower Store, Inc.), Andrew
and John Boschetto and Joseph Murphy (Boschetto's
Bakery, Roslindale), Patricia Boudrot (Filene's Base-
ment), Gerard Burke (Doyle's), George Burkinshaw
(Ye Olde Pepper Companie), Joseph and Charles
Callanan (Roach's Sporting Goods, Inc.), Cambridge
Historical Society, Jeffrey Cirace (V. Cirace & Son,
Inc.), Elizabeth and Frank Forest Davidson (Long's);
Paul Davis (Davis Monuments), Rupert Davis and
Dan Cianfarini (Schoenhof's Foreign Books), Edward
Caniff (W. C. Caniff & Sons, Inc.), David and
Andrew Demeter and Anthony La Chapelle (Chelsea
Clock Co.) Bartolemeo De Stefano (Boschetto's Bak-

ery, Boston) Matthew Deveney (Deveney & White Monument Company), Nevart Dohanian (Bon Ton Rug Cleansers Inc.), Edward Fitzgerald (Quincy Historical Society), Ellen Fitzpatrick (The London Harness Company) Edward Flynn (New England Flag and Banner), Samuel Ellenport (The Harcourt Bindery Inc.), Peter Englehardt and David Walker (Shreve, Crump & Low); Michael Finn and Steven Vaughan (E. B. Horn), Kevin Fitzgerald (Jacob Wirth), Beth Ann Gerstein (The Society of Arts and Crafts), Kenneth Gloss (Brattle Book Shop), Roger M. Griffin, Kathleen and Robert Shure (Giust Gallery), Len Goldstein (Keezer's), David Grossberg and Renee Garelick, (The Colonial Inn), Deborah Holt (J. J. Donovan's Tavern), Stephen Joyce (B.L. Makepeace Inc.), Seana Kelley (Durgin-Park Market Dining Rooms), Guy Le Blanc (Longfellow's Wayside Inn), Susan Redgate (Copley Society of Art), Daniel Lourenco (Phil's Barber Shop), Patricia Holbrow Long (Holbrow's Flowers Boston, Inc.), Paul MacDonald (Leavitt & Peirce), Ann Maestranzi (Charles W. Benton Company), Kathleen Melley and Joanne Hilferty (Morgan Memorial Goodwill Industries, Inc.), David Marks (Stoddard's) Paul E. Murphy Jr. (M. Steinert & Sons), Adam and Geoffrey Muther and Glenn Pratt (E.R. Butler & Co.),

Marianne Mileno (Union Oyster House), George Moriello (George's Barber Shop), Lynn Paget (The Swan Boats of Boston), Louis Paltrineri (James F. Fiske's General Store), George Papalimberis (La Flamme's Barber Shop of Harvard Square), Paul Parisi (Acme Bookbinding). Eugene Pierrotti (Bent's Cookie Factory), Allan Powell (Harvard Coop); Lewis Russell Jr., (Russell's Garden Center) Scott Samos (Martignetti Liquors), Roger Saunders (The Lenox), William and Andrew Schell (Schell Printing Company), Katherine Shepard (New Balance), Rob Skolnick (E.A. Davis), Holly Smith (The Boston Society, David and Theodore Stoia (Boston Lock & Safe Co.), Michael Swartz (Swartz True Value Hardware), Edith Toth (The College Club of Boston), Scott Vanderhoof (Vanderhoof Hardware Company), Edward Ver Planck (Dickson Bros. Co.), Abbot W. and Robert C. Vose III (Vose Galleries), Alan Weiss (Wm. S. Haynes Co. Inc.), Robert Eldridge White Jr. (Robert E. White Instruments, Inc.) Stephen L. Willett and Steven Smith (L.J. Peretti Co., Inc.), Don Wilson (Wilson Farms), Barry Zimman (Zimman's Inc.)

For their assistance, I also wish to thank William H. Brine, Barbara Burg, Bridget Cooke, Nicholas Daniloff, Will Holton of Northeastern University, William A. Davis, Robert and Barbara Day, Frank and Marianne Durgin, Louise Erdman, Ilse Fang, Danguala Gabis, Charlotte Hall, Janice Hunt, Carol Lodi, Colette Manoil, Patricia Maroni, the National Park Service, Beatrice and Peter Nessen, Robert Oppenheim, Nancy Peace, the Social Sciences Department of the Boston Public Library, Carol Stocker, Frances Tenenbaum, Christina Tree, Penelope Uhlen-dorf, Henny Wenkart and Chris Wallace.

ABOUT THE AUTHOR

Phyllis Méras, the former travel editor of the *Providence Journal*, has a long acquaintance with Boston, both from her days as a student at Wellesley College, and later, as editor of its alumnae magazine. She is the author of fourteen books. She is a year-round resident of Martha's Vineyard.